SKIN TO SKIN

SKIN TO SKIN
Eroticism in Dress

Prudence Glynn

New York
Oxford University Press
1982

First published in Great Britain by George Allen & Unwin, Ltd., 1982
First published in the United States by Oxford University Press, Inc, 1982

ISBN 0-19-520391-7
Library of Congress Catalog Number: 82-81091

Printed in Great Britain

CONTENTS

List of Illustrations and Acknowledgments   *page 7*

1 You Could Go Naked   15
2 The Feminine Ideal   28
3 The Peacock's Tail   58
4 The Short Haul to Hypocrisy   82
5 Getting the Message   108
6 Shared Secrets   122
7 Let Rip   136
8 Perilous Pleasures   145
9 Future Imperfect   153
  Index   156

ILLUSTRATIONS AND ACKNOWLEDGMENTS

COLOUR PLATES

Between pages 48 and 49

The power of Paris chic (National Magazine Co.)
The British contribution to erotic dress (National Magazine Co.)
The relaxed Italian attitude to fashion (National Magazine Co.)
The American dress of overt power (Rex Features)
The intimate sublety of French couture (Vogue France – George Hurrell)
Cretan goddess (John Decopoulos)
'New machine for winding up the ladies' (Mansell Collection)
Zandra Rhodes by David Remfry (David Remfry)
Jayne Mansfield (Kobal Collection)
The commonplace and therefore unerotic breast (Homer Sykes)
The Cannes Film Festival (Homer Sykes)
The immense erotic significance of the top of the thigh (Daily Telegraph Colour Library)
Captain Marryat's adventures (E T Archive)
Marilyn Monroe in *Let's Make Love* (Kobal Collection)
The S-bend in the modern idiom (Camera Press/Charlotte March)
Lady Diana Spencer (Rex Features)
The gipsy look (Rex Features)

Between pages 96 and 97

Stance (Homer Sykes)
What does the small waist signify in men? (Jean Loup Charmet)
Frederick Gustavus Burnaby (National Portrait Gallery)
Adam Ant (Rex Features)
The Establishment way with colourful dress (Homer Sykes)
Napoleon enters Berlin (Jean Loup Charmet)
'Pour une jupe trop courte' (Jean Loup Charmet)
'Ecclesiastical Scrutiny' (British Museum: photo Eileen Tweedy)
'Parisian Ladies in their Winter Dresses for 1800' (Ray Gardner)

See-through, spring 1980 (National Magazine Co.)
The Frill (National Magazine Co.)
Modern Venus arising from the waves (National Magazine Co.)
Botticelli's 'Birth of Venus' (Scala)

Between pages 128 and 129

Samson and Delilah by Van Dyck (Dulwich College Picture Gallery)
How to Marry A Millionaire (Kobal Collection)
Erotic dress in advertising (Sanders)
The ad-man's fantasy (Dormeuil)
The corset in 1830 (Leonard da Selva)
Lingerie of 1919 (Jean Loup Charmet)
The wrong place at the wrong time (Triumph International)
Lingerie for display (Syndication International)
Political underwear (Jean Loup Charmet)
Classic eroticism in dress (National Magazine Co.)
The scarlet women (Sanders)
Swiss national costume (Mansell Collection)
The press-stud (Philippe Maille)

BLACK AND WHITE ILLUSTRATIONS

	page
Poke bonnets (BBC Hulton Picture Library)	16
Lady Settrington by Lord Settrington	17
The first examples of erotic dress (Mansell Collection)	18
The Queen of Punt (Peter Clayton)	20
The Pilotello Line (BBC Hulton Picture Library)	20
Sheila Ming (The Times)	21
'A Devilish Fine Woman' (BBC Hulton Picture Library)	23
Mother Hubbards	23
Perfection in the female form, 1895 (Kharbine)	24
Modern street erotica (Homer Sykes)	25
Madame Wilcote of Northleigh (Mansell Collection)	31
The bound look by Karl Lagerfeld (Associated Newspapers)	33
Chinese foot-binding (Popperfoto)	34
'On the road' (Mansell Collection)	35
The 'maid' shoe (Ian Murphy)	36
The eternal contradiction in dress (Camera Press)	37
'The Jealous Old Man' (Giraudon)	38
Jean Harlow (E T Archive)	38
Thunderthighs (E T Archive)	41
The mini-skirt (Camera Press)	42
Patterned tights (Keyser)	43
An honest woman in the Métro (Jean Loup Charmet)	44
The neck and spine in the Far East	46

	page
Monroe's stand-in, 1956 (BBC Hulton Picture Library)	47
Hot pants and jogging shorts (Rex Features)	48
Cleopatra (BBC Hulton Picture Library)	49
Hair at its most ridiculous (BBC Hulton Picture Library)	50
The beehive (Popperfoto)	50
Ritual hairdressing (John Topham Picture Library)	51
Punk hair-dos (Homer Sykes)	51
The allure of the shoulder (BBC Hulton Picture Library)	53
Long gloves (BBC Hulton Picture Library)	54
The long 'swan' neck (John Topham Picture Library)	55
The 'civilised' version of the ringed neck (National Magazine Co.)	55
Indian carving from the second century AD (Victoria and Albert Museum – Crown Copyright)	56
The conqueror (Mansell Collection)	59
'Clothes Maketh Man' (Mansell Collection)	59
The chairmen of the major banks (Rex Features)	61
King's Road teenagers (Homer Sykes)	61
Decorated phallic symbol (Susan Griggs Agency)	62
The hooded executioner (Pacemaker Press Agency)	63
Solid tradition (Popperfoto)	64
'Aesthetics' by George du Maurier (Mansell Collection)	65
'Why Not?' by Charles Dana Gibson (Mansell Collection)	66
The 'Anatomical principal', 1829 (BBC Hulton Picture Library)	67
'Corset contre l'Onanisme' (Jean Loup Charmet)	69
Underneath the kilt (Reid & Taylor)	69
The Emperor Augustus (Mansell Collection)	70
Charles V by Titian (Mansell Collection)	71
George Washington, by Horatio Greenough (Smithsonian Institution)	72
Statue of Roman general (Mansell Collection)	72
Classical armour as fancy dress (Mansell Collection)	74
Bjorn Borg acknowledges his worshippers (Sport & General)	77
American footballers (Syndication International)	78
The allure of the trucker (Robert Estall)	80
J. R. Ewing (BBC Pictorial Publicity)	81
Richard Chamberlain as Dr Kildare	81
Henry VIII's codpiece (Crown Copyright)	83
Investiture of Prince of Wales, 1911 (Syndication International)	84
Investiture of Prince of Wales, 1969 (Syndication International)	85
Emperor Bokassa, temporary king (Rex Features)	86
Louise of Lorraine (Mansell Collection)	87
Duke and Duchess of Connaught (By gracious permission of HM the Queen)	87
Glory of three kinds (The Times)	88
'The Wheel' by Callot (Mansell Collection)	89
St Jerome (Bibliothèque Nationale)	91
Gabrielle d' Estrées and the Duchess de Villars (Rush/Sibert)	92

	page
A mish-mash of ancient and modern (Rex Features)	94
'Fashions of the Period', 1883 (Mansell Collection)	95
The most decent indecency (BBC Hulton Picture Library)	97
'Masquerading' (BBC Hulton Picture Library)	100
Duke of Connaught in fancy dress (By gracious permission of HM the Queen)	100
The ladies Churchill as Watteau shepherdesses (National Library of Scotland)	101
See-through (Rex Features)	102
Virginia Wade (Syndication International)	103
Gamages swimwear parade, 1925 (BBC Hulton Picture Library)	104
Topless swimwear (Camera Press)	105
The modern equivalent of Iphigenia (Rex Features)	106
Female sacrifices to male paying-power (Homer Sykes)	110
Martyrdom of St Teresa (Mansell Collection)	112
Page 3 pin-up (Rex Features)	112
Making love fully clothed (Victoria and Albert Museum – Crown Copyright)	113
Vulnerable innocence (National Magazine Co.)	116
Hollywood fantasy costume (National Film Archive)	117
His Girl Friday (National Film Archive)	118
1895 advertisement for 'lumière reglée' (Jean Loup Charmet)	120
1900 advertisement for bicycles (Jean Loup Charmet)	120
Mural surrounding clothes shop window (Rush/Baitel)	121
Nudity to sell motor cars (Homer Sykes)	121
Advertisement for Elliott boots (John Topham Picture Library)	121
Typical nude calendar (J. John Masters)	121
'How extraordinary!' (Jean Loup Charmet)	123
Crinoline hoops (BBC Hulton Picture Library)	123
The 'Specialité' corset (BBC Hulton Picture Library)	124
Elaborate underwear of the 1920s (BBC Hulton Picture Library)	125
The whirlpool bra (BBC Hulton Picture Library)	126
Idealised undies	126
Lingerie for lingerie's sake (Harvey Nichols)	127
Art overcomes the risks of exposure (Mansell Collection)	129
Tattooing (Homer Sykes)	132
Tribal markings (Alan Hutchison Library)	132
Apollo chases one of the Muses (British Museum)	137
French 'redingote' (Mansell Collection)	137
André Courrèges (John French Photo Library)	139
Fastening for fastening's sake (Atomage)	140
Easy on, easy off (Rush/Baitel)	141
Girls as luggage (Camera Press)	141
Apparently easy prey (Rex Features)	142
Slashed garments (Mansell Collection)	142
Spiral zip (Michel Haddi for VIZ Magazine)	143
Perseus and Andromeda	146

	page
The Martyrdom of St Agatha (Mansell Collection)	147
Potentially suffocating dress (Atomage)	148
The dilemma of pain and pleasure (British Museum)	149
Lock up your daughters (Rex Features)	150
The Alternative Miss World Competition (Homer Sykes)	151
Hermaphroditism (James Palmer for ID)	151
Victorian soft porn (BBC Hulton Picture Library)	152
'Les Batteuses d' Hommes (Jean Loup Charmet)	152
Cuirasse by Paco Rabanne (Rex Features)	154
Something to wear down to the disco (James Palmer for ID)	154
Modern snake dress (Polly Hope)	155

SKIN TO SKIN

1 YOU COULD GO NAKED

THIS IS not a book about 'dirty' clothes, nor is it a 'dirty' book about clothes. It is a fashion book which poses the somewhat unusual question as to why you, gentle reader, are wearing anything at all as you riffle the pages or indeed why the author did not sit stark naked at her typewriter (actually she was most usually at work in her dressing gown, which matches the herbaceous border – but even if it did not, there are those who find appeal in the slob). Prosaic persons will reply that the reason why we still dress and generally adorn ourselves is that an awesome amount of money is invested in the textile and cosmetic businesses and that it would not be in the interests of a powerful body of citizens – merchants, creators and manufacturers – were we not to do so.

The commercial reply has many justifications, even if a cloud of bankruptcies and the rather turgid general state of the textile industries of the world in the 1980s suggest that many of the efforts of this lobby have been misguided.

This book, though, suggests a quite different motivation for the fact that you are not reclining in the privacy of your own home *tout nu* for your reading, or at most tossing a drab blanket over your shoulders on your way to the public library in nippy northern climes in order to take out your copy of *Skin to Skin*.

Skin to Skin springs, fully armed as Minerva from the head of Jupiter, from the conviction that Robert Burton was right, that 'the greatest provocations of our lust are from our apparel'. Which means that everything can be boiled down to sexy dressing, and that if we

15

A caricature from around 1820 which emphasises the import- ance of dress as a sexual lure when the face and hair are out of fashion as erogenous zones. Although the drawing is greatly exaggerated, as are all the best cartoons to make their point, this particular style must have given rise to as many misunderstand- ings and mis-sightings as the cloche did a hundred years later: 'I can't remember the face but the shape is familiar.'

still have a wardrobe of clothes instead of just the useful blanket it is because Eros, god of love, depends from every coathanger, be it coin-op cleaners' wire or hand-made, padded and scented. He always has, although – or because – his disguises are infinite.

Throughout all ages and regions, man, and even more so woman, has used some eight areas of specific sexual arousal via the intellect in observing dress. The presentation of these eight, however, has proved as intractable as I believe it to be enlightened because an impersonalised tome, working methodically from hair to toe-nails, would by definition be impossible. Every single item of clothing which I have included could feature in many chapters as having a quite different significance to each. Equally, many items of clothing which might be expected to occur – genital jewellery perhaps? – do not, because while I can see that having your decayed teeth filled with gold and gems is quite funny, the concept of having your private parts pierced, your labia or penis assaulted, your nipples dug out, seems to me as unerotic as having your cheeks stuck with safety pins or your ears bored until in late life the lobes droop, horridly, towards your neck.

Beginning then with the belief that optional dress is selected to provoke the crucial clash of two parties to produce a third, the eight

16

isolated areas would be: blatancy; innocence and vulnerability; protective power; overt virility; intimacy; determination to survive through conformation; the priming of the hunting instinct; and sexual arousal through danger.

Whatever the means of dress employed, the outcome should be the same: the sexual gratification of at any rate one of the parties involved. But since I have elected to analyse the wearer rather than the garb, it follows that every piece of clothing can crop up in any of the sections under scrutiny. Codpieces and corsets, Snow White puff-sleeves in the society salon or the brothel, women in trousers allowed into conventional settings (how long before men in frocks will be, too?) – all crop up in these studies as tightly interwoven as a yard of Yorkshire worsted. Can it be coincidence that the Gay Liberation Movement and the dress it prefers can get out of the closet only when societies find themselves fully populated? Forcible authorities hell-bent on war and conquest of territory or mind take grave exception to sexually sterile dressing.

In its final form, *Skin to Skin* has required not so much objectivity as subjectivity in writing. While dutiful authors and sensible publishers no doubt prefer that the adjective 'definitive' can be skewered somewhere on the dust-jacket blurb, if you start from the premise – which then is borne out by research – that practically anything mankind wears has stimulated somebody, somewhere, it follows that an attempt to be definitive about so fleet-footed and witty a subject as dress will be dated before it reaches the bookshelf. Histories of hemlines apart, one has in the end to opt for an angle on dress, and make it an acute angle at that.

I therefore make no apologies for editing in a highly personal way the aspects of eroticism in dress which I have chosen to include. Written by a man, this book would, I suspect, be an entirely different proposition but I am (a) not a man and (b) prone to the theory that when men start writing about dress they plump for well-documented authority, have never sat in the front row at Dior and, worst, too often lose that crucial irreverence with which fashion reporting must be spiced if it is not to die as surely as a frock in a museum.

Thus although I suppose most readers who expect *Skin to Skin* to be concerned to a very great extent with the clothes adopted by women since these might be assumed to be more consciously erotic in their appeal, I have written as a woman who observes the sexes without discrimination but who always prefers the subtle to the obvious. Caveat emptor: I have devoted as much speculation to the lure of the three-piece suit as I have to black suspenders.

Unlikely though it may seem, Christian religious painters of the fundamentalist persuasion were responsible for the earliest record of

The sexy hat which draws attention to the head rather than obliterating it. As the silhouette of clothes for the most part staled in the 1970s, there was a predictable rise of interest in accessories such as hats and shoes. Designed by David Shilling (and photographed by Lord Settrington, the grandson of a Duke), this picture of a girl who could be anyone until you see her face (in fact, Lady Settrington) reverses the message of Les Invisibles, in which the face mattered nothing, the body all.

17

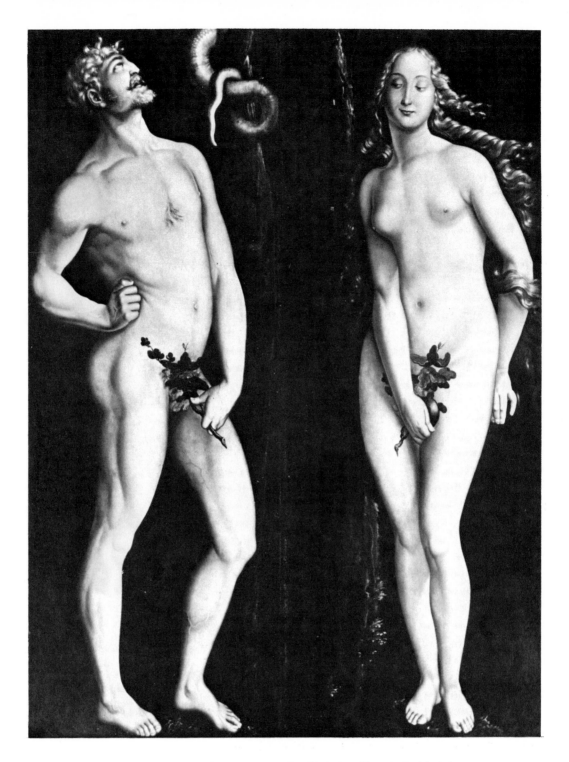

The first examples of erotic dress. The Christian Church decided that the genitals were unacceptable reminders of human frailty, and inculcated a guilt about sex which still lodges in many hearts today. Eve has noticed that Adam has got something that she has not but is already preparing to take advantage of the situation by crossing her legs. Baldung, who painted this picture, must have had a fine sense of humour, for Adam's curls are already teased into a semblance of the cuckold's horns — or are they the horns of Pan? Darwinists would have painted him with a chest wig.

erotic dress. In all their works depicting the Garden of Eden, a fig-leaf covered the genitals of Adam and Eve the moment that they stopped wandering about in hermaphroditic innocence and the apple was transformed into breasts for the lady, testicles for the man. Since all this took place in a climate where presumably wearing anything at all was unnecessary, the paintings instantly produced the thought that there was something shameful or unwarrantably exciting about certain parts of the anatomy.

In Western culture that shame and erotic stimulation still tends to linger on the sexual organs but the Bible, which is open to as many interpretations as an utterance by the Delphic oracle, has something for everyone since in some interpretations for 'fig-leaf' you can read 'leaves', that is the produce of the entire tree, held together inexplicably but covering up all sorts of bits of Adam. This may explain why different cultures, while adhering to the general principle of spontaneous combustion of man by some superhuman power, feel quite at ease when revealing bits of themselves which might make others blush. The part played by God in all this can best be described as enigmatic. 'Who told you that you were naked?' he enquired, and it is tempting to think that his tone of voice was rather that of somebody who has only to turn his back for a minute after six days' hard labour to find that someone has been making mischief.

Anyway, God duly provided fur coats for the by now embarrassed pair, but here again the interpretation is questionable. Fundamentalists say that the furs were those of other creatures and were applied to hide the unacceptable wickedness of the bare human form. Upholders of the Darwin theory of evolution explain this growth of hair as nothing to do with modesty but a practical precaution taken by a naked ape when he began to move to less idyllic climes. Millennia later, he is naked again, except that having got hooked on the way by the Fundamentalist view, he now mostly wears clothes or snatches some other creature's dress.

The totally irreverent, of course, hold that when God saw that everything he had made was wonderful except for these bald pink blobs like new-born mice, he determined to do something about it right away and to leave them to sort out why for themselves. Since the whole world is still arguing, it was quite a good ruse.

What cannot be disputed is that man is one of the few species with the leisure and inclination to 'improve' himself bodily, to actually change his shape. He is the only species to attempt to improve on Nature by however cruel a course. This is linked to the fact that, almost uniquely, the female is permanently available for mating purposes. While many animals and birds and even plants exhibit exotic and presumably erotic dress, and the blue-behinded ape

which skips upon the trees of Paradise (Eden, so where was *he* when the prudes were handing out the fig-leaves?) has no problem in enchanting the lady ape at the right moment, man is continually on the sexual hunt. There is no close season, and thus intense and unending competition between the one sex in pursuit of the other.

So as soon as his life consisted of more than just running after his dinner and ensuring the continuation of his type, man turned his attention to making himself more attractive than the next man, and his efforts to change his shape range through discomfort, mutilation, distortion, decoration, risk to life and health, covering and uncovering. The only justfication for so much time and trouble must surely be man's libido.

Ideals of beauty in both men and women have varied through the centuries and in different cultures. In 500 BC or thereabouts, the

20

What is beautiful has always been open to changing views. In very poor communities, fat is beautiful because it denotes the ability to provide not just necessities but food to excess; it is a taste which is still appreciated in underdeveloped countries. This Egyptian relief of the Queen of Punt (far left), as well as being the earliest example of the S-bend, shows flabby lumps of flesh which make modern obesity problems seem modest in proportion.

Left: What was known as the Pilotello Line, and it certainly does have overtones of an ocean-going boat – all stem and stern, with a prow to plough through the roughest seas and a wake of ruffled train. 1903, the date of this picture, saw the beginning of the end for the S-bend, because a great many women were already in revolt against this unhealthy and unnatural stance which presented a woman walking like an ostrich, and equally finely plumed.

The beautiful Sheila Ming (right) in a John Bates swimsuit in 1978. The posture is in fact the same as that of the Edwardian woman but in this case the pose is natural and athletic, and she looks more set for running off if things don't go her way than for feigning the vapours for the same reason.

Egyptians, a lissom and elegant people, were astounded by the fatness of the wife of a middle African king. For his part he, coming from a poor country, would have thought fatness in a woman lovely, betokening as it did her rank and wealth. A 'good' figure has included the strange, thrust-forward stomach and backward stance of the fifteenth century and also the exact opposite, the thrust-out chest, pushed-back pelvis and protruding bottom of the late Victorian age. In the middle of the seventeenth century beauty was voluptuous and loosely dressed, yet a hundred years later a graceful, tall body was admired. Next there was a brief return to a liberal interpretation of 'classical' dress, then a long reign of artificial doll-figures, then looseness was admired again, until in our own time there is no one set pattern of style in beauty and it has become every woman's (or man's) right.

21

But ideals of beauty are not the same thing as erotic dress, even when dress plays a large part in achieving those ideals. Erotic dress is dress which has as its basis the deliberate intention to stimulate – either others or the wearer – and it is with this aspect of 'fashion' that this book is concerned.

Erotic means 'of love', amatory (which can be platonic), or sexual (which can be anything). If you accept the Fundamentalist point of view, or believe what you read in Freud, it is possible to assume that all dress is erotic in that it conceals something which by tradition is not acceptable to the public gaze. Inquisitive as he is, and prurient by nature, it follows that man has always been excited by what is concealed. It is always what is underneath which must be discovered, which goes a long way to explain why, in an age when clothing is largely unnecessary for survival, warmth, status or decency, men and women still fill their leisure moments to such a degree in dressing and undressing themselves or one another.

It was not until the eleventh century that a pattern of dress cutting was evolved which enabled the hitherto straight lengths of cloth, variously draped, to be shaped into the body. Once the secret of shaping garments was out, there was no telling where man's vanity would stop, and from that date onwards what has been regarded in dress as disgraceful, open to arrest, acceptable, elegant, boring or wildly exciting has varied as widely as the cultures, climates and centuries in which man has had access to a change of natural shape.

Very roughly, the major influences on erotic dress may be divided into four sections: religion; the state and the law; the media of communication; and Society at large, in work or leisure. Once again, the variations within these groups as to what is proper and what is 'erotic' are enormous. In the first instance, religion, one has to compare motives as disparate as chalk and cheese. While Cretan priestesses and Indian religious figures concentrated on fertility at its most luscious, aided and abetted by clothes which would rank now as fetish items, it was the Christian Church which was first to condemn the waisted cut of the eleventh century and to pronounce this early attempt at haute couture as the work of the Devil. It has always seemed to me a delicious irony that the good missionaries, horrified that the savages they had been sent to convert were running around quite happily and innocently with nothing on, may have introduced the notion of erotic dress instead, with all its excitements, by shoving what they considered wicked behind a cotton shift: the fig-leaf and the Mother Hubbard are closely related.

The sexual implications of who wore what have long been a source of worry to those in authority, as is witnessed by the many statutes, laws, controls and punishments imposed on clothing at different

22

'A Devilish Fine Woman' runs the caption to this picture from 1836 (above left), making a pun with the slang of the time, in which 'devilish' was a compliment, and re-iterating a complaint which had been made since medieval times, namely that ultra-high fashion was the work of Satan. Unfortunately, since Satan had not been sighted for some eons, the artist of this cartoon against vanity presents a tame set of devils. With no forked tails or snappy sets of horns, this unconvincing bunch look like flayed cats.

Above right: The hideous cotton shifts imposed on the hitherto innocently un-dressed natives converted to Christianity by missionaries in Africa were called Mother Hubbards, from the nursery rhyme of that name: 'But when she got there, the cupboard was bare.' The imposition of concealing clothes has the same innuendo as the fig-leaves of Adam and Eve (see page 18). Suddenly, what had seemed quite natural was made to seem wrong. But what is covered is always more exciting. . . .

times. Since Authority is always highly sensitive to economic considerations and to the pressures of Society such as the size of the population and the availability of that population's livelihood and lebensraum, its reactions in acceding to or ignoring circumstances are extremely interesting.

The most powerful factor in breaking down the taboos on erotic dress has undoubtedly been the communications media. With the

23

dissemination of knowledge comes the imposition of alien values, values which may be highly critical of either the excess or the lack of explicitly sensual adornment as shown in art and real life. Thus it took the early package-tour leaders to decide that the paintings at Herculaneum were not suitable to be communicated to a mass audience, while the magnificent carvings on Hindoo temples are discreetly by-passed by guides, who explain away the magnificent phallic symbols as lightening conductors. Such things had been admired and enjoyed by centuries of independent and sophisticated travellers, but such independence and sophistication in sexual matters is generally alien to the Masses, with whom the media are mostly concerned. Nor do the Masses on the whole have much sense of humour about erotic dress; the Few, who do, would be more likely to study such stimulating art from the attitude of envy, having a nasty suspicion that if they tried out similar postures similarly clad they would stand a good chance of breaking a leg.

The Greeks have a word for it but have failed to provide the picky modern market with what it wants to buy in terms of erotic dress. Paraphernalia means, in literal terms, all that a woman could legally claim as her own before the Married Women's Property Act of the late nineteenth century and is defined as personal articles, wearing apparel, jewellery – anything for show and decoration. The French have no word for it but they provide it just the same. Oh dear, I hear you yawn, not another lengthy polemic about why Paris is the fashion capital of the world. No, not quite that, but facts are facts. Optional dress makes all the world your oyster, while economic and social forces dictate that the recognition of this speeds a desire for somebody to package the whole tantalising but jet-lagging mess under an authoritative stamp. With China and Russia both stripped of their exoticism and their ethnic dress, and with Japan exchanging its highly specialised form of sartorial allure at about the same rate as its cars penetrate the Western markets, four countries, Italy, Britain, America and France, can be seen both to demand and to provide clothes which meet the specifications of some of my eight suggested areas of *volupté*. Only France supplies them all.

Paris remains Mount Olympus in fashion terms. Names come and go on the little gilt chairs and on the invitations which warrant a tick in the top right-hand corner. Just as Olympus harboured many divers gods and sub-deities, not by any means all pleasant or agreeable, so Paris draws a pantheon together. Is it something in the atmosphere? I am not acquainted with Mount Olympus save from a somewhat smudged photo in the *Larousse Encyclopedia of Mythology*, where it bears a marked resemblance to some hill in North Wales

Perfection in the female form as viewed in 1895. This is a window-display model, available with or without articulations, 'pour bicyclettes and costumes vélocipèdistes'. The head was an extra, but then who cares about heads with such a divine body?

24

enduring Bank Holiday weather, but acquainted with Paris I most certainly am.

Paris in its collections is never derivative, though it is frankly osmotic, absorbing the stronger saps from all over the world in order to burst into bloom yet again. The greenhouse has certainly sprung a few leaks over the years, but while the other major powers in dress provide one colour on the palette, Paris provides the spectrum. In Paris, fashion does not vainly flap her tinselled wing, she Concordes off to the markets of the world. Paris can give authority to outfits which while created in Britain would be laughed aside on home ground, Paris can emulate the robes of cardinal and king. Like all surviving rulers it massacres (discreetly) unruly elements, fights off competition, provides for heroes and for circuses as well as for the sexually insecure and the socially beleaguered. The two can come very close. What more calming, for example, than a Balmain label when the media hound you to find out just why your husband ditched all to marry you.

France generalises; other countries specialise. For example, Italian clothes have always been more overtly seductive, more languorous, prettier and generally much more fun than those of the French. When Charles VIII of France went a-warring into Italy in the fifteenth century, he and his followers were astounded by the beauty and refinement of lifestyle and above all by the sense and use of colour of their neighbours, in such sharp contrast to the coarse, cold, grey castles they had left behind. The French gawped and absorbed, taking back with them far more than battle honours, a transformation of their view of beauty and of the proper way for persons to decorate themselves and their abodes. Indeed, the great French textile centre at Lyons was founded on the Italian example. In the sixteenth century a Medici bride and her entourage so ravished the French court with the splendour of their dress that it seemed politic to offer consumers a similar home product rather than let all that good money flow out of the country.

Italian fabrics are still greatly sought after because of their sexiness of colour, of touch, of novelty. The fact that your order for cloth may never arrive and that the expense of every metre seems enough to rouse Venice from the sea probably only adds a necessary ingredient, danger, to the heady cocktail which Italy mixes. But Italian designers of the silhouette, Schiaparelli, Pietro Cardini (Pierre Cardin) or Valentino have been absorbed into the Paris cell. Pucci, Fortuny, Missoni remain essentially Italian because the allure of their work relies largely on what the clothes are made out of.

The British, enmeshed still in their romance with every other part of the globe save their own tight little island, make clothes for

Modern street erotica: sawn-off jeans, bateau-neckline T-shirt and high heels. The top is scarlet, the pants the requisite denim. Plenty of bosom, the hint of a sexy bra under that cheapie shirt, to judge by the angle of her bust, and all that long, dark hair and pouting expression. No wonder that the man behind is risking being run over by a truck.

25

dreamers, romantic in the extreme, lusty, brave, fantastic in the truest sense, definitively original, impractical – and sexy. The dress of colonisers, pirates, confident loose-livers. England was never noted for womenswear until the mid-1960s, menswear having held the world in thrall to the classy upper-crustiness of the latest rulers of most of the globe. The reason that English dress for men was copied with such avidity was because it exemplified a lifestyle of aristocratic eccentricity or plodding wealth.

American designing is still dominated by social insecurity. Beautifully made, well priced or colossally priced, perfection is what is sought in whatever price bracket. I have never forgotten wearing a new, very tight, black skirt, much shorter than the current vogue outside New York, in the late 1970s. Thinking it a touch dull, I nipped open the back seam five inches so that when I walked, the skirt would flirt a little leg. But being careless and European, I neglected to turn away the silk lining from the slit, so that when I walked there was indeed a peek of the untoward.

'Sew it up at once,' hissed my English escort, well versed in American life. 'They'll think you're poor. They can't take clothes as a joke yet.'

Paris would have thought the tip of my lining quite delicious, and the most marvellous opportunity for a little sympathetic help.

The American contribution to eroticism in dress, though I doubt that they recognise it, is in precisely this area of total perfection. Theirs is the dress of power and privilege, as befits the most prosperous and expansive nation on earth. 'Power is always fashionable,' wrote Alistair Cooke, commenting on the inauguration ceremony of President Ronald Reagan and musing in particular on the super-smart style of wife Nancy in her 'adorable' little red hat. It came as no surprise, after so shrewd a journalist had selected a fashion angle for a major broadcast story, to learn that indeed Mrs Reagan has allocated three whole bedrooms at the White House to her wardrobe.

It is eroticism of the least direct kind, but it is of exactly the type which appeals to Americans, who on the whole tend to be very proper and very formal in what they wear. As Bernardine Morris of the *New York Times* has remarked, 'Americans will accept junk food, but not junk clothes.' They are simply not turned on by sloppiness, and that slight touch of the slut which holds a fascination for some European men is abhorrent. The Puritan ethic and the residue of the pioneer days is still to be observed in their style. The men must be impeccably tailored, their women pure and doll-like and band-box fresh (preferably wearing gloves). It is what I call the apotheosis of WASP dressing. Try buying a career-girl suit in London in 1982 and the chances are it will be by the American designer, Calvin Klein, and even though it was made in Hong Kong it will set you back several wage packets at our lowly rates of pay. But by the time you read this the career-girl suit will have truly arrived, for with the opening up of America to Europe by cheap air travel, America will be the most potent source of changes in lifestyle and dressing for the European continent.

2 THE FEMININE IDEAL

Ever since man discovered that through the medium of clothes he could change the shape of the species with comparative ease and with comparatively little discomfort, he has used this knowledge to transform 'fashion' into a long-running game of sexual hide and seek. Now you see it, now you don't. Man's low threshold of boredom with his own appearance and that of others pushes him to diligent and ingenious experiment with the exposure or the mysterious concealment of various parts of the body.

When life was lived at a more leisurely pace, or conversely in harsh times when there was little opportunity to do more than fight for survival and in any case the options on dress were extremely limited, these changes in areas of special erotic significance were slow and inclined to be regional rather than global. In accelerated modern life with its mass communications bringing thoughts from virtually every region, its much heightened expectancy of length and its vast resources in textile terms, the process of change, and with it the roundabout of significant points of interest to the opposite sex, has speeded up. Indeed, during the twentieth century alone, practically every silhouette in dress and practically every inch of the body has been quarried to provide new material for excitement.

One obvious result of the quickened pace of style has been the virtual disappearance of bodily mutilation, which not only takes a very long time to achieve and may cause intense pain or even malfunction to the body, but which takes even longer to undo, if indeed the process is reversible without recourse to major surgery. Since the introduction of structured clothes permitted the appearance of change without the necessity of having to opt for a permanent

28

'beauty' which might in time come to be regarded as a hideous deformity or an unacceptable social practice, only two areas of the anatomy have been subjected with regularity to the mis-application of dress to the extent of physical damage. These two areas are the waist and the feet. It will hardly come as a surprise, therefore, to learn that it is these two long-suffering areas which have proved the most consistent and the sharpest erotic prods in the wardrobe.

Although the turnover in erogenous zones has almost kept pace with inflation in the Western world, one factor remains constant. It is that almost without exception only one point of interest is revealed at a time, it effectively douses the thrill engendered by its predecessor. The swings of choice have been quite spectacular, there being moments when the very thought of a bosom or a leg caused yawns of ennui, and others when it brought orgasms of excitement.

Men of course have erogenous zones too, but they have tended to be less diverse and to remain more constantly appreciated, so I intend to consider masculine attributes in the next chapter, which is specifically devoted to the ways in which they have sought to make themselves irresistible.

When a man did make a great effort it was as likely as not to please himself, to impress his peer group or in pursuit of sheer lust. It is mainly women who were (and in many cases still are) the primary subjects of sartorial experiment. It is clear that until very recently – within the last twenty years – the main burden of pleasing by presenting an attractive and sexually arousing image was carried by the female, in direct contrast to the laws of the animal kingdom and certain primitive peoples. It is worth considering both why this is so and, more importantly, the influence women themselves have had on the distribution of their charms. On the surface it might seem that they were but gratifying the whims of their dominant partners, but I would not be so sure.

Women were for centuries little more than possessions of men who literally did rule their world. Not to be found attractive to a man was the ultimate humiliation. Nor did the snags stop there: the fecundity time allotted by Nature to women was less generous than that enjoyed by men. Ah, you say, but who cared about fecundity? Surely more mouths to feed was the last thing you wanted, especially if the mouths might not be of your own begetting? And surely older women can be as alluring and even more satisfactory as sexual partners? After all, was that not proved by Madame de Maintenon, mistress of Louis XIV, who complained at the age of seventy to her Confessor that sex three times a day was really a bit too much, and could she not plead a few headaches? (The answer was, 'No, lest the King get into mischief elsewhere.')

The key is that the allure of possessing a woman capable of bearing a child is as old as mankind itself. It is dyed into our religion, law, social mores and heaven knows what else besides. It is rooted in medical history, in the days of huge infant mortality rates, of bad feeding and of hard work causing the female reproductive processes to wear out even faster than they do now, in the myth of super-virility implied by a large number of children to one's credit, and in the practical consideration that there would be plenty of young labour for the farms and plenty of hands to keep you in old age.

It is also worth remembering that even with the shortage of men brought about from time to time by wars or by everybody going off to discover new bits of the earth, what men were around were well able to impregnate as many women as the law would allow or as boldness suggested, and having impregnated them to abandon them until they had given birth and were thus trim and fully available again. So the competition among women really was tough, and it is hardly surprising that the dress which excited men with normal sexual desires, which induced risks even, which ensnared the necessary protector, was frequently that of youth and fecundity.

Hence the brilliant concept, undoubtedly thought up by women, of permitting only one charm to be worshipped at a time and, when that charm seemed to be getting a little over-exposed, moving to another to revive flagging interest. Thus they spun out the years of fascination for as long as possible, diverting the eye from any sign of ageing, keeping the 'hunter' ever alert for new sexual game. They dressed to kill and to keep their claws well into their prey, a neat reversal of their apparent rôle which proves women subtle when it comes to turning necessity to their own advantage.

It is only fair to say that women have been aided in their scheming by men, especially those men with an empathy for the female psyche rather than a lust for her body perhaps, and all but a handful of the truly great makers of clothes have been men. That the change wrought by dress can be dramatic in the battle of the sexes we have on the authority of the late Christian Dior, who was quoted as saying that you could never alter a woman's style unless you altered the man in her life. It is tempting to wonder whether there were moments, say after a particularly exasperating fitting on a particularly shapeless customer, when the gentle but hard-headed M. Dior pondered the feasibility of turning his dove-grey salon into a discreet house of assignation – after all, a lot of fun and games had gone on in the fitting-rooms of the haute couture at the turn of the century.

Indeed, in Paris to this day there are women who enter into a passionate conspiracy with their dressmaker, hairdresser, shoe-maker, lingerie boutique and beauty parlour in order to retain their hold on a man. Doubtless this happens in other cities too, but it must be admitted that just as French men are more receptive to chic and more appreciative of its finer points, so are French craftsmen and craftswomen particularly sympathetic to these vicarious liaisons, regarding a success as a triumph for their work, a failure as theirs, too. Somehow it is hard to conjure up quite such an intimacy with a health gym or a cosmetic surgeon.

These women are not, as you might think, creaking relics of another age. Many are young, beautiful and very successful at what they do. And what do they do? They please men, quite deliberately, and one of their greatest weapons is dress and the multiplicity of rôles which it enables them to play in order to appeal to whichever taste in erogenous zones is manifested by their partner of the moment. Now that 'types' have taken over from a universally accepted 'fashion line', no girl has to wait around any longer for her best attributes to come back into style, she just accentuates them now.

The rest of this chapter deals with the outward and visible signs of dress in highlighting specific portions of the body at various dates.

The waist

If you watch, the first place that ninety-nine per cent of men will touch a woman when indicating more than a formal courtesy is on the waist. In friendship or devoted love, his arm enfolds her waist as the couple wander off into passages of Tennyson, or the doughty champion scoops her to safety. With more specific sexual desire, a man will lightly run his palm down her back and dip, literally, into her waist at the point where he can feel the start of the swell of her hips. Grown bolder, he will grasp her to himself around the waist first.

The waist is the one erogenous zone which has never gone completely out of fashion even if it has been apparently by-passed by the outer layer of clothing. The waist was the one area which women – and men – longed to display and it is no surprise therefore that it is the invention of a cut of dress in around AD 1000, which allowed fit in place of straight or slung drapery, which can be seen as the first example of erotic fashion.

The reason for the endless fascination with the waist is that it symbolises virginity. If you consider it, the one area which, left unconstricted, is proof of childbirth is the thickened waist. All other proportions of the body may regain their original shape, but there is always some loss of the maidenly trimness through the centre of the body (frequently a slight curve to the stomach, too, which no amount of dieting or massage can entirely remove, for it is something inherently to do with posture).

By the start of the fifteenth century the Church had so far accepted the idea of waists that they allowed your effigy to be preserved in a very smart manner. In fact, this waist is a compromise because it clearly belts under the robe at the back and only emerges for the front half of the body, a fashion which was revived most recently by Paris in the late 1950s. With her sly, blank eyes and bee-sting lips, a spread eagle on the middle of her hat, gloves with at least thirty buttons apiece and six rings on each hand, Madame Wilcote of Northleigh in Devon, England, exudes power and elegance.

To give an example: a girl who at the age of eighteen had a waist measurement of twenty-two inches might, after the birth of two or three children and without wearing constricting garments, expect to have a twenty-eight or thirty-inch waist measurement. This is also why fertility symbols are frequently shown with tiny waists which prove them still in good nick for providing offspring and which are made to appear smaller still by swelling thighs and breasts.

The constriction of any part of the body can stimulate sexual desire in both wearer and observer. In the case of the waist, some women undoubtedly felt a frisson from knowing that their suffering was the object of admiring glances and aroused protective feelings. It has often been argued that more recently men were so excited by a small waist no longer because of its antique connotations of nubility, but obscurely through a jealousy that they themselves could not bear children and thus achieve matronly curves except with old age and over-eating. So they demanded that their women should have slim, even dangerously slim, waists, and to goad their sex subjects to extremes they themselves wore corsets – garments which in shape are much more suited to the masculine physique, by the way. The turn-on was presumably the knowledge that the women were suffering at their command, were endangering their health perhaps, and were at any rate partially immobilised: the prey could not escape.

Ancient civilisations show a marked divergence in their dressing of the waist. Thus in China, Greece and Rome, robes of both men and women were loose and flowing. However, among less civilised societies and especially among peasant communities which were less blasé and more superstitious, the waist was constricted from the earliest records of dress or bodily adornment. Examples of this may be found in the culture of Ancient Crete, and in the peasant dress of almost any European country.

Western society, however, has placed great emphasis on the waist. Only three periods of fashion could be seen as neglecting it: the late fifteenth century, when a strange stance raised the juncture of bodice and skirt to close below the breast; the Regency period, when a chic return to what was deemed classical dress produced the same effect; and after World War I, when ideologies had taken such a battering that Society seemed hell-bent on demolishing as many sexual differences as possible in dress.

The foot

After the waist it is the foot which has been subjected to the greatest degree of sexual attention and the greatest degree of pain, deforma-

At the Paris ready-to-wear shows in October 1981, the Press got very excited about the rediscovery of the waist. Any social commentator or indeed any fashion commentator with a grain of prescience would have seen it coming a year before. With not enough jobs to go round, a woman must be kept in her place, and even if these days that place is not always, in the immortal words of James Thurber, 'in the wrong', it's certainly at home and not with her chin one rung up on the company promotion ladder. The best exponent of the bound look is Karl Lagerfeld of Chloé.

Westerners frequently express horror and disgust at the idea of the bound Chinese foot. Physically, since the mutilation was begun at birth when the bones are very soft, as with the moulding of the skulls of infants by certain tribes in Africa and South America, the child may have suffered little. Perhaps, therefore, it is the psychological implications which alarm. Ironically in view of corsets and other devices, this particular instance of tampering so drastically with the shape that Nature intended for no other reason than vanity, or rather in order to render the victim more pleasing to and dependent on the male, affronts the Christian mind. The lotus-foot shoe was seldom more than four inches long. The deep, fleshy crevice obtained by binding was seen – and used – as an alternative vagina.

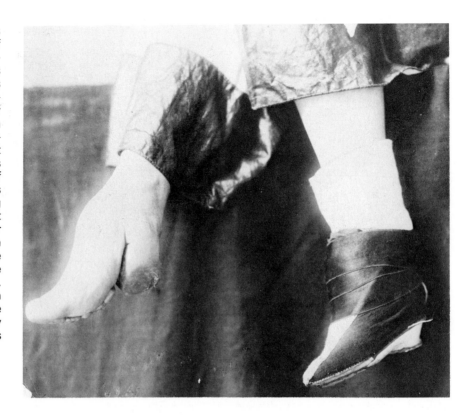

tion and ill-health from what it has been obliged to wear. In some cultures the size of the foot is equated with the size of the vagina, the principle being that small is beautiful. It also has connotations as an alternative penis, and indeed it is sometimes used as a polite word for genitalia. Podocoitus, the penetration of the vagina or other orifices with the foot, is frequently referred to. Both Chinese and Indian art depict this or that famous hero having sexual intercourse with five women at once, two of them via his feet, and in Italy a large phallic object is known as the big toe of St Cosimo.

The most extreme examples of foot worship were to be found in China, where at one time a foot which was not deformed was a dishonour because it suggested that the woman was not utterly the subject of her husband's domination and prepared to illustrate her devotion to his pleasure by her own discomfort. In the wider context, the tiny foot, squeezed until very recently into always too-tight and very unkindly-shaped shoes, continued to be an object of excitement all over the world. Tiny feet meant class, leisure, fastidiousness. Who wanted some great clod-hopper?

History is so redolent with foot fetishism that it is interesting that at any rate in open conversation it is the part of the anatomy which most observers claim to find the ugliest naked. Certainly modern feet

34

ON THE ROAD.—A GLIMPSE INTO OTHER PEOPLE'S TRAPS AS SKETCHED FROM THE TOP OF OUR DRAG.

are, or were until recently, hideously deformed by 'fashionable' shoes, a price paid willingly it seems, as willingly as any deliberate deformation such as that practised in China. Is it fear of the magically erotic power of the naked foot, which modern man cannot quite understand, and which has not been a subject of a learned lecture or a programme on BBC 2 with accompanying manual? Or is it that some secrets must remain, and that with so much else laid bare the exquisitely shod foot, foolish, impractical, buttoned, bowed, thrusting the calves and pelvis into the most provocative positions, is just so much more exciting?

But men have been prepared to suffer equal discomfort, and if a small foot was admired in women, it was just as much a vanity peg for men. A well-known shoemaker alleged that even today his private clients always order their shoes to be made too small, which poses an interesting analogy between East and West. In the Western woman a small foot is the sign of delicacy, vulnerability and the need for protection; in the East it is the sign of gentle birth, and has no effeminate connotations.

Although the feet are quite extraordinarily erotic parts of the body, and without doubt women's feet are vastly exciting to men, men's feet are primarily exciting to themselves, on the narcissistic or fetishist planes. To many men their feet are deeply sensual. One extremely successful and handsome American man described to me his disappointment in his first pair of London hand-made shoes – an ambition of his life, like getting a hitherto inaccessible woman into bed – as 'a sexual débâcle' because he did not like them. In Budd Schulberg's famous novel, *What Makes Sammy Run?*, the nearest the ex-New York slum Jewish boy made good gets to orgasm is when he

On the other hand, the same effect as that achieved by Chinese foot-binding – although in a somewhat less drastic form – has been admired over the centuries. Compare the pushed-up instep, the tiny pointed toe (with its phallic connotations) and the height of the heels on these bottines, c. 1871, with the Chinese deformation. 'I don't love you 'cos your feet's too big' goes the jazz song; or, on a more refined note, 'Her feet beneath her petticoat like little mice stole in and out,' wrote Sir John Suckling in the seventeenth century. To have big feet is to be a clodhopper, a common person, and so to this day women voluntarily deform their feet by wearing too small or impractical shoes.

35

A work of art, a work of craft and quite the sexiest shoe to come out of 1980. Named 'La Bonne' (the maid), this glimmering black patent-leather pump has a high heel moulded to resemble a woman's buttocks and legs, poised tippy-toe. A glacé kid apron bow, perforated to resemble the broderie anglaise trim of real maids' uniforms, adorns the heel of the shoe, giving the impression of a woman bending over. The vamp is outlined in white kid, and the vamp has an apron on it in white, neatly tucked and frilled. The shoe is by one of Britain's outstanding designers, Thea Cadabra, and the heel sculpted by her collaborator, sometime jeweller James Rooke.

has fifty-six pairs of hand-made shoes. No doubt they were very tight, too, to make the feet look small, to conceal all those years of having to run around after others.

What is so extraordinary about this desire on the part of men for a small foot to denote leisure after a life of toil, a privileged, dainty foot which has never walked anything but its own acres, is that women frequently judge the likely size of a man's phallus by the size of his feet. So what is the man with small feet trying to tell you now? Is this why the rough end of the homosexual world, off-duty fighting men, salesmen calling on lonely housewives and a certain sort of film hero all have to wear vast shoes? Does the dream created by Hollywood costume extend to padded lasts?

Because of the sexual implications of the foot, its revelation or concealment has been the subject of varying codes of modesty. Because of its position at the mobilisation end of the leg and thus its association with the ability both to run away and to enhance the stature of the wearer to the possible detriment of the male, the female foot has frequently been forced to adopt clothing which has effectively made movement extremely hard and slow, acting in the same way as a shackle or fetter. High heels and thick soles have been the object of laws and much social discussion, yet women's attitudes to freedom of feet, when offered, can be very ambivalent. As recently as the 1970s, platform soles allied to shorter skirts illustrated this point. Not prevented by their dress from running away, women chose as a high fashion shoes which deleted all but the most sober gait.

The breasts

Possibly no area of the female anatomy has aroused such intensely ambivalent feelings as the breasts. In the view of Society, Authority,

Right: The eternal contradiction in dress, which has an eternal appeal. The girl on the right, tall, blonde and pretty, is wearing the minimum permitted in the street, apparently demonstrating her liberated womanhood and all set to flee any unwelcome advances. But look at her feet. She is wearing the modern equivalent of the chopines of the Venetian whore of earlier centuries. Chopines in Venice reached extreme proportions, sometimes twenty inches high, but despite the efforts of the authorities to make the wearing of such dangerous shoes illegal, women persist in the desire to be taller and thus more noticeable to the predator, while at the same time giving themselves no chance of flight. Ironically, the girl on the left, although hobbled to the ankles by her dress, is probably less vulnerable in her espadrilles, but then the sexual message that she is sending out is a quite different one. Platform soles were revived by high fashion as the 1970s dawned, but speedily sank to the mass market and particularly the ethnic minority groups. Again the authorities had to step in, banning such shoes from school lest the pupils break their necks between classrooms.

The cross-your-heart method of lifting and separating the breasts goes back a long way, as this detail (above left) from the eighteenth-century painting called 'The Jealous Old Man' by Boilly shows. Jean Harlow, the reigning sex queen of the silver screen in the 1930s (above right), had an elemental lure, less dizzy than Monroe's, and a type of good-natured toughness which she shared with Mae West. She, or at any rate her dressmaker, knew all about lifting and separating. Those who are picky about their couture might criticise the seams on this particular gown, but who cares? The goddess is come among you.

the media, but above all as an erogenous zone, the position of the bosom has been a trembling one. Alternatively essential, to be pursued and ravaged, or to be completely obscured or exposed only to indifference, the bosom has also been a focus for intense jealousy and particular spite.

Women's breasts are said by myth to be the two halves of the apple from the garden of Eden. Another apple, or other bits of the same one (it may after all have proliferated like an amoeba), were used as the testicles of Adam. If you follow this line of thought you must reach the inevitable conclusion that women have just as much sticking out in the way of sexual attributes as have men. Was Freud therefore wrong in his theory that every single woman is born with and frequently never loses penis envy? Or is this the reason why men fundamentally resent these female attributes and seek either to exploit them or to suppress them? If the more there appears to be of you – so long as it is in the right places – the more important you are, it could appear that women are as much in evidence as men. That they have hardly if ever thought so is illustrated by the remark made by Queen Elizabeth I, a pillar of liberated woman power: 'Had I been crested' (i.e. had she had a penis) 'instead of cloven' (referring to her own pudenda), 'you would not have dared to treat me thus.' So she definitely felt she had a physical lack. In fact, this is all the more interesting taken in the context of the belief that the Virgin Queen had a physical aberration about those parts or that she might in fact have been a hermaphrodite.

However it is the maternal aspects of the breasts which supply the most material for the study of the part they have played in the shifting cycle of sexual stimulation. At their most fundamental, the breasts suggest security, maternity, warmth, comfort and food: a delicious spongey tactility, the warm remembered smell of milk perhaps, the suggestion of plenty and satisfaction. The breasts indicate generous bounty without the threat of having to perform anything more difficult than sucking. (The vagina is a much more threatening target, requiring as it does a distinct physical change on the part of the attacker if it is to be put to proper use or even fully enjoyed by both parties.)

The men most attracted to large breasts are often either insecure and seeking a mother figure, or rumbustious and attracted by such overt feminity and its suggestion of fertility. In sophisticated eras the bosom is much less in demand, but as soon as Society feels itself insecure or under pressure the larger bust is returned to favour.

Periods at which the breast has been considered delicious or charming (as opposed to being an erogenous zone highlighted by dress) coincide, as one would expect, with the periods when they have been openly on display, whether for the commendable purpose of breast-feeding, or just because nobody was particularly turned on. Thus sixteenth-century Venetian courtesans revealed all above, indeed it was a mark of their profession; seventeenth-century English court beauties left little to the imagination and neither did the chic eighteenth-century French coquette. In medieval times, both Church and State permitted the uncovered bosom: martyrs, madonnas, fashionable ladies and allegorical figures in art popped out nipples and unlatched bodices all over the place. Victorian prudes saw nothing wrong (or so they said) in having flimsily garbed Virtues, usually 'restraining' prancing horses, jumping around the walls of their Civic Halls – even in Scotland.

On the other hand, the Edwardians were shocked by breasts (they were interested in bottoms and shoulders) and inserted little stuffed cushions so that the cleavage could be formed into a mono-prow.

It took the arrival on the civilisation (European and points East, that is) scene of the Puritan Americans to re-establish the breast as wonderfully erotic. Complete with all the psychological hang-ups about the frankly physical nature and use of lots of bits of our anatomy, by the time their wealth and power was such as to impose a style on the world, they were a bottle-fed, not a breast-fed nation. An innate yearning for the natural 'milky fount' has been suggested as the cause of America's obsession with bust sizes. Sterile bottles and plastic teats cannot compare with the touch and smell of living flesh, with all its failings.

Most interestingly in terms of dress, this yearning, which is implicit in all those sweater-girl pin-ups and cantilevered co-eds of the late 'forties, came at a time when, for once, American fashion dreams had been cut off from Europe. Left to themselves, American designers majored in on the bosom and GIs, sent not to Paris but to remote islands where native lovelies showed their almost all, yearned to see those same curves covered up, as they had yearned to see Mom's curves accessible. With a neat irony, it is an American ex-movie star (films were the first shock wave the Old World had to swallow in bringing in the New Bosom), HSH Princess Grace of Monaco, who has, from her Gallicised home, been prominent in the revival of breast-feeding in Europe.

So the Americans, wielding both novelty and dollars to say nothing of their seemingly unending determination that all is possible if you work at it, certainly changed the shape of women in the media. Incidentally, they must be held responsible for the arrival of the truly exquisite La Lollo on the adolescent consciousness of a generation of flat-chested girls; well, the Italians have always been quick to exploit a solid native attribute.

But Paris was different. Italy succumbs, Paris dictates. After some suitably feminine curves as arranged (iron-clad, as Mom had been) by M. Dior in the guise of the New Look, about as formidable as the *Graf Spee* to attack, Paris told all these wealthy hicks that breasts were just not classy. By the early 'sixties exuberant hoe-downers had returned to their anxiously smart stores with the news that the bust was out. By the time (1968) that Yves St Laurent, their god of European style, had given it the ultimate snub of showing it under a transparent blouse with an ambiguously hermaphrodite outfit – shorts, blazer and bare chest – everyone knew that the message was: Tits? So what?

By the 'seventies TV personalities such as Esther Rantzen were suckling in public, and even the galleries of the Royal Academy of Art in London had been observed in the diary of its trendy president as being a location for the same activity.

The legs

For a very long time, legs were reserved for men as displays of

40

erogenous excitement, although as we have seen, what is not revealed is just as exciting if cunningly presented. The reasons why men got a start on women in the display of nether limbs were, first, practical. They had to ride, they had to fight, they had to walk, in short they had to move, all activities which were severely if not dangerously impeded by long, flowing skirts. Women on the other hand should show their dependence, vulnerability and immobility by being hampered as much as men demanded; men's freedom of action compared with the inaction enforced by long skirts gave endless opportunities for gallantry.

Since the concealed is so exciting, the long skirts also provided an almost endless game of trying to peek. The outer clothes might reach

Only one name for this lady: Thunderthighs. Weighing in at a guess at around two hundred pounds, this rounded pin-up of the late nineteenth century has not missed out on one trick: frills, thonged shoes, ultra-deep stocking-tops, jewellery on a naked breast which she is wisely supporting by the classic dodge of putting her hands behind her head. Pin-ups are for drooling over, so it is as well to capture a wide audience.

A picture which says more than words can about how the wheel of fashion brought the legs into prominence again as an erogenous zone with the introduction of the mini-skirt.

to the ground, but if they could in some way be rumpled, or caught up, or disarrayed in the dance or in a riding spill or, in the classic piece of hypocrisy, by the girl allowing her lover to push her on a swing, what naked delights might not be glimpsed.

The inside of the upper leg has the most delicate and sensitive skin. In the erotic novel, *L'Histoire d'O*, the girls are whipped there to induce special pain, and this fact explains the excitement of stocking tops with their band so specifically outlining, protecting and compressing this most erotic area.

It took two wars of global proportions to reveal the legs of the women of the world, and fashion, being a tease as it always is, no sooner had let show the hitherto secret mechanics of female perambulation than it decided that they were boring, and skirts grew longer again.

Free legs are of course an outward and visible sign of the freedom to move about economically, socially, geographically, and therefore they constitute quite a challenge. It is interesting that the nation

42

But the mini-skirt which promised such hitherto unrevealed delights turned out to be a bit of a frost save for those who just like legs per se. Voyeurs, who imagined that women were silly enough to give all away at once, peered up escalators only to find that while under a long skirt women were prepared to wear stockings and frilly panties, the moment that skirts rocketed upwards in tune with the new technology, tights were born; all you could hope for was a peek of a wrinkled gusset. Tights did at least provide a new canvas on which designers could express themselves in elegant patterns such as this herringbone design which flattered and drew attention to the newly revealed nether limbs.

which has always shown the greatest interest in the quality of the undressed leg is America. This is because it is one of the only civilisations in which women started off on a much more equal footing with men, and even the entrenched pioneers with their old traditions bred a liberated race. American men gaze in awe at the Atalantas they are persuaded that they ought to pursue, although in much American society it is arguable which of the sexes is the prey and which the predator.

For centuries women, unless goddesses, fertility symbols or performers, seem to have been supposed to move on castors. Things reached the height of absurdity in the latter part of the nineteenth century, when not even pianos were allowed to have un-knickered supports and when, in carving the roast bird, it was not permissible to mention any preference more specific than light (breast) or dark (leg) meat. Men, however, had every chance to show off their manly calves in unergonomically tight armour, hose and full-dress uniform trousers.

43

A quoi en est réduite . . .

une femme honnête . . .

The introduction of the Métro, or underground railway system, to Paris at the turn of the century, while responsible for some magnificent art nouveau ironwork on the outside, was also the source of some heart-searching among respectable women who wished to avail themselves of this popular service. The juxtaposition of their handsome behinds with a jostling mass of travellers, who could explain a little pinching by the swaying of the carriage, needed to be considered. 'An honest woman is reduced to this to travel with impunity on the Métro,' reads the caption to this 1901 cartoon.

. . . pour voyager impunément dans le métro.

The back and bottom

In the middle of the 1960s, when coloured model girls first made a real impact on the fashion media, one fact immediately became apparent: they were not the same shape as the white lovelies who had dominated the catwalks hitherto. Not only were the coloured girls not the same shape as their traditionally Aryan counterparts, they were not even the same shape as one another. Such however was their beauty, their originality of movement, their mysterious exoticism and, perhaps one should not forget, their mostly very newly-won acceptability in the upper echelons of Society and style, that their inclusion in a smart show was irresistible. The combination of trendy political awareness and a spice of erotic presentation of clothes which jabbed some flagging designers into new life was a useful amalgam of high, liberal thinking on a most commercial level.

The main distinction between the new wave of model girls and their predecessors could be phrased succinctly by saying that what the latter carried in front the former carried at the rear. The prow gave way to the stern and some very tricky fitting problems it made for, too. Instead of the standard-size group who could at a (literal) pinch be popped into a dress destined for another identikit mannequin when something fearful happened to the running sequence, such a practice now carried the threat of painstakingly measured creations arousing catcalls from the audience by being too long in front and hoicked up behind. Provocative? Possibly. Chic? No.

But then, since we have already argued that the essence of dress is stimulation, it is not surprising to find that the arrival of these exquisite if uniquely formed creatures quickly brought about the discovery of new erogenous zones for fashion to explore. They were the back, and the bottom.

According to the psychologist, Bernard Rudofsky, 'Some tribes discriminate in their admiration for obesity between over-all bulk and specific, strategically placed cushions of fat. The most celebrated among salient features is steatopygia, the overdevelopment of the subcutaneous fat that covers a woman's hind parts . . .' The illustrations to this thesis clarify the point made earlier about the change of preference from prow to stern. The ladies chosen to show their charms have by Western European standards small, low-slung breasts, far from the perky Lolita or luscious Mae West image, while that area inadmissible in the model agencies' tape-measured books sticks out like a shelf for a tea-tray. Buttock-lovers, again according to Rudofsky, 'make their selection by ranging their women in a line and picking her out who projects farthest *a tergo*'. Buttock-lovers, it

45

The neck and spine have a particular erotic appeal in the Far East, where women tend to be small-breasted. They enhance this charm by the traditional hairstyle, in which the hair is scraped up off the neck into an elaborately decorated chignon, thereby adding apparent inches to that delicate area covered with the nerve-ends which make the back a source of pleasure for massage. Almost everyone likes to have their back scratched.

should be added, are frequently found among those who prefer sexual penetration from the back, hence the predominance of steatopygia among un-Christianised peoples. This may be responsible for the adoption of the term, 'missionary position', i.e. penetration severely from the front, reducing the natural sexual charms of the woman to a flattened pancake, when alien sexual practices were imposed in the name of propriety and godliness onto a submissive culture.

The erogenous place of the spine is more subtle and elusive. It is therefore not surprising to find that it plays a major part in oriental eroticism. In very highly sophisticated and leisured cultures, the art of stimulation reaches the most delicate heights of intellectual abandon. Again, dress is the message-carrier, the aspect of appearance which signals to the sexual partner. Thus in Japan, while every kimono is cut away from the back of the neck and from the collar bone, the precise degree of what it reveals is very precise indeed. For a married woman or for a high-class daughter of the house, the cunningly stitched padded rim will set off her head and neck like a flower in a vase, ready for the man to pluck, but at the same time the knowledge of the spine, the core and supporter of life, is a privilege merely suggested by the costume. For the geisha, the professional courtesan, the kimono stands right away from the neck, which is as heavily lacquered as the face and which is as erotic in its symbolism of the flower which may be taken. But the kimono of the geisha is cut so that as she kneels, her lord and possibly master may glimpse right down to her tail-bone – and bliss beyond?

In Western cultures the back, as used as an erogenous zone by fashion, never surfaced except in the most intimate circumstances until the progeny of Empire and slavery achieved a degree of liberation in the mid-1960s. From then on softly draped jersey dresses, exemplifying the influence of Japanese designers, became a major factor in ready-to-wear collections. The space-age couture, denied its traditional feminine qualities of bosom and with the legs relegated to tights-clad underpinnings, found the primeval curved spine and the inviting lips of the bottom newly stimulating. The back was bared and accentuated by the cutting and stitching of fabrics or the use of lace.

The bottom has had three spectacular revivals since Nature suggested it as fashionably interesting. Most extraordinarily, and surely as no result of the conquest of and knowledge of the obscure races, the Edwardians suddenly stopped being circular Victorians and adopted the *droit-devant*, a hideously uncomfortable, low-breasted, stomach-repressed, bum-stuck-out silhouette. Commonly called the S-bend, this precarious line was supported by padding and drapery and appealed to the sated appetites of the overfed society.

The next revival came fifty years later and should be attributed for convenience's sake to one feminine idol – Marilyn Monroe. With her, the wiggle was back, the impossibly short step on too-high heels was back, but the stunning thing about Monroe was that she combined the best of the West and Africa, having both a spectacular, GI-approved prow and a native bottom which would have had the drums beating with or without the missionaries. The outerpinnings of her triumph could hardly have been more simple: demure, little-girl frocks from which her far from little-girl figure protruded in apparent innocence, or a skin-tight sweater dress.

There followed a period in which the bottom was relegated by fashion to anonymity (as indeed was much of the figure) by the sweeping draperies of the flower children and the back to nature print-smock, but the pause in interest was a short one because along with all this worthy thought came cheap travel, greater leisure and mobility. Ethnic drapes were all very well when it took three days to get by mule-back through the Peruvian mountains or whatever, but they were awfully flappy to handle for stand-by jet travel. Blue jeans were re-born. The first were baggy, durable and worthy, as had been their ergonomically sound ancestors in the genre. The difference was

In 1956 the famed *Picture Post* photographer, Slim Hewitt, shot this memorable backside picture of a girl called Una Pearl who was Monroe's stand-in for the film, *The Sleeping Prince.*

After a period of decorum, hot pants and now jogging shorts have done for the bottom as an erogenous zone in dress what Yves St Laurent did for the bosom — they have made it just too obvious, and so non-erotic.

that now jeans did not need to be nearly so ergonomic. At a guess, only a small proportion would now be required for such things as homesteading in Wyoming, bending double all day panhandling for gold, or knocking together a few railroads. And so jeans became a fashion item, and the more fashionable they became the tighter they got, so tight indeed that some medical opinion feared for the safety of the vital organs so enclosed.

The bottom was back, though it was not to receive the brand of high-fashion approval until the spring of 1981, when the Paris collections revived the bustle. Yves St Laurent made the point exceptionally clear by sweeping black crêpe tightly around the hips and finishing it off in a big bow. For good measure the skirt below was split up the centre back to mid-thigh.

48

For all the talk of women's liberation and their determination to be comfortable and not to play up to the wishes of men, in 1980 Karl Lagerfeld of Chloé, with all the power of Paris chic behind him, could still persuade women to tighten their belts. Dining rooms around the world were filled with exquisitely dressed ladies pushing the food around their plate and hoping to distract attention from the fact that the only thing they had room to eat was an indigestion tablet, so tightly were they bound.

The British contribution to erotic dress has always consisted of two elements which at first sight are mutually incompatible: it provides on the one hand the strictest tailoring, with all its exciting disciplinary overtones, and at the other end of the spectrum a wonderfully romantic dishevelment. Fashion has never been a particular pre-occupation of the British, who, regarding themselves as superior to other mortals on the whole, wore what was suitable in their view. This tended to comprise sporting clothes as they galloped about the green and pleasant land by day, and soft pretty dresses, made from fabrics which were the spoils of an Empire, as they waltzed in their superb country houses. Zandra Rhodes exemplifies this throw-away sense of privilege, as the creation above shows.

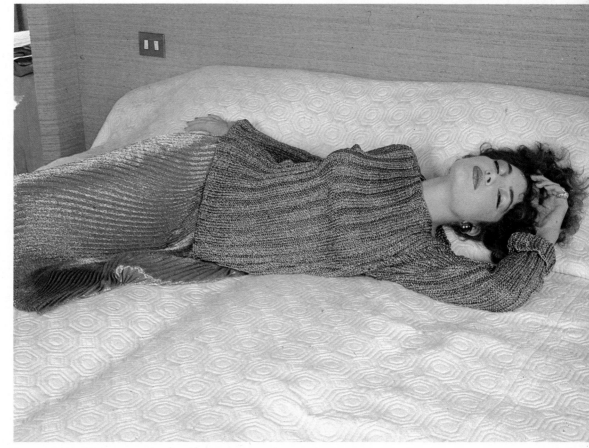

While the French stun with dramatic chic, the Italians have always taken a more relaxed attitude to fashion, relying very much on fabrics for the appeal of the garment. Colour, tactility, textures: all contribute to make Italian clothes quite different. The lines are usually supple and fluid, suggesting the body beneath instead of imposing an alien silhouette upon it. Italian men, women and children spend a great deal of time thinking about their appearance and wondering how to improve it with none of the inhibitions about vanity or expense which beset other races, and they are intensely aware of their surroundings and their light. They do approach dress with a sense of humour, though, and with great confidence, so it is not surprising that it was the Italians who made knitting a world, not cottage, industry. Italian knit-wear is a by-word for sensuous luxury and imaginative use of textures and threads. This design is by Krizia of Milan from their collection for winter 1980.

Since Americans lack a long enough tradition of gracious living to back up their belief in their own taste, it comes as no surprise that the admired dress in America is the dress of overt power, which means of perfection, of outward materialistic success. Of course this attitude is softening around the edges but even in 1981, President Reagan's wife, Nancy (above), was always impeccable and band-box fresh, having so obviously taken a great deal of trouble to please her man and to present the proper image of the consort of one of the most powerful men on earth. She therefore represented a great turn-on in fashion, particularly to men who are struggling up the ladder (or are simply married to sluts).

The intimate subtlety of French couture at its peak is shown in this dress by Hubert de Givenchy (right). Outwardly a simple sheath made in an animal print which was popular in 1980, the wearer and her couturier know that every single stripe has been sewn on by hand, that the stripes are deliberately arranged to raise and accentuate the breasts and that on the mount of Venus the stripes come together, oh so by chance it seems, to a neat hole in the pattern. Long, tight sleeves suggest the thoroughbred limbs beneath; access to them is made easier, but only for the chosen man, by a long zip down the back.

A CORRECT VIEW OF THE NEW MACHINE FOR WINDING UP THE LADIES

Everyone got very excited as the 1980s dawned on a recessive world because fashion had rediscovered the waist. But has it ever been away, except for those heady days of the 1960s when the pill and going to the moon seemed alternatives to life on this planet and fashion blanked out the natural female form? The Cretan goddess (above) with her towering hair, inflated upper half, minuscule waist and burgeoning hips has much in common with the nineteenth-century caricature of a young woman submitting to the demands of fashion (above right). The goddess was a symbol of fertility, but is not the same true of this portrait by David Remfry of Zandra Rhodes (right)? Snakes as accessories apart, and given the puffed sleeves in place of the naked puffed breasts – they provide the same silhouette – it does seem to be a case of 'plus ça change'. Since the goddess is robed to the floor, though, it is impossible to determine if, like Zandra, she is wearing classical laced sandals. A guess would be yes.

Nowadays you just buy a balloon woman and inflate it till the proportions match your individual taste in shapes. The late 1940s, however, were less sophisticated in their technology and it was still correct to pin up photographs of the women whose physical statistics, duly emphasised by the fashions of the time and the guile of the media, made up the stuff of dreams for millions of men. Jayne Mansfield, the American actress (main picture left), epitomised the pneumatic though real charms demanded by homesick GIs. The defeated Italians got their own back later by producing Gina Lollobrigida, whose busty charms gave an inferiority complex to the other half of Europe.

By 1980 (inset left) the breast had become commonplace and therefore unerotic – indeed, in this picture, aesthetically really unpleasing. Not much dreaming to be done about what you will find when you get this particular lady into your sticky embrace. Ironically, the page of the magazine facing the one that engrosses her is a bra ad.

Society, or rather the more raffish section of it which patronises show-biz events such as the Cannes Film Festival (above), does not want to miss out on any aspect of eroticism in dress, and usually turns the shocking into a joke. Yves St Laurent had demolished the breasts as an erogenous zone in 1968 by showing his notorious see-through blouse. Women more clever just kept covered up unless what they had to reveal was of such classic perfection that it transcended accusations of indecency.

The top of the thigh has immense erotic significance. Not only does it suggest to the viewer that 'Heaven's above', or 'You're almost there', but it is also an area of particular texture in the skin, very sensitive and vulnerable. Hence the allure of broad, black stocking-tops (below) which signalled to the unlucky the no-go area. Admirers found many ways to peek at the unpantied charms, the most famous being getting the lady to swing on a swing (immortalised in the picture by Fragonard) or to romp about and get knocked down (by mistake of course), as in many illustrations by artists such as Hogarth. The upper thigh lost much of its appeal with the invention of knickers and suspenderbelts, which put it more into the 'discipline' area of eroticism.

Puzzled which to Choose !! or, The King of Tombuctoo offering one of his daughters in marriage to Capt. ___ (anticipated result of y^e African Mission)

The bottom line. Marilyn Monroe (right) offers bosom, tummy and backside to a selection of admiring sexes in the film, *Let's Make Love*, with a wiggle that has a real tribal thump about it; while the gallant explorer, Captain Marryat, on his mission to Africa in the early nineteenth century (above), gets offered bosom, tummy and backside. An interesting sociological note is that while Monroe, one hundred and fifty years later, is obviously in command of the situation and the watchers are lucky to be able to be there, the dusky ladies are very much on the receiving end of affairs. Note that both Monroe and the princesses go in for a lot of teeth-showing, too.

The S-bend in the modern idiom (left). No need for corsets – the body says it all quite naturally with an unconstricted waist, the buttocks thrown up by high heels and a very sexy sway to the spine. With her small, boyish bosom, emphasis on the spine and shoes which render her submissive, the 1980s Western girl is much in the Oriental tradition.

One of the most provocative teases is the dress which looks as though it might fall off. It was to be found in prudish societies when practically everything else was covered and teenage misses were chaperoned by aunt, governess or Mammy round the clock, but if a bright admirer could induce a giggle or a sigh there was just a chance of a slip in the corsage. In peasant societies it still exists, though in these the penalty for causing an unexpected revelation would be not social ostracism but being pitchforked or knifed by dour male relations. High fashion recalled the bare-shouldered look in the early 1950s, along with the modified crinoline, but those dresses were about as liable to fall off, boned to perdition as they were, as an Olympic show-jumper. In the mid-1960s (below), a much more sexy and sympathetic interpretation of the off-the-shoulder look was around amid a raggle-taggle of gipsies, some couture, some not, but it took the nineteen-year-old Lady Diana Spencer, stumbling out of her unaccustomed low-slung limo on her first public appearance with her husband to be, the Prince of Wales, and clutching at the most incongruous dress which very nearly did fall off (left), to remind men all over the world that what apparently stays up can also slip down.

The hair and the head

Everybody gets very excited about the rôle of hair as an erogenous zone, probably because it is so involved with virility and because of its creepy ability to grow, like toe-nails, after death. Certainly hair has shot into and out of the erogenous limelight as many times as most bits.

Understandably, hair is always most important when the silhouette of clothes is dull. If you are stuck with your chiton, robe or plaid, and unversed in the neat arts of couture, hair remains a great area for fun and games. When undressing a member of the opposite sex revealed not really very much more or less than was expected from the outer carapace, the mystery of the hair and the make-up remained to haunt the speculation of the conqueror. In all probability the most sophisticated lovers were content to leave the mystery intact and to enjoy its subtlety, its beauty and the artistry which had gone into its construction, while taking a more active enjoyment of other corporal delights. Modern man, however, has been brainwashed (or rather more aptly hairwashed) into thinking that long, or at any rate plentiful, thick hair is an essential for attractiveness and that he, like his women, must live out his twenty-fours with a coiffure through which the admiring fingers may at any moment be riffled. Thus for many a man sexual foreplay is an agony of suspense lest his toupée should come ungummed.

Long hair has of course its very own excitement, especially when it is pinned up elaborately or whimsically. The elaborate style challenges the unknotting of this glorious veil (and how much of it is hers, anyway?) and the vulnerable wisps, skewered in with random hairpins, leave the lover of long hair trembling for the moment when the whole lot falls down, probably to the force of gravity but, to his ecstatic gaze, in submission to his own fascination.

In Western Europe since what one might call the dawn of fashion, hair has spent most of its time in hiding, possibly because this made it even more exciting when it was revealed. Prosaically, but more probably, hair, like the teeth, was usually dirty, smelly and lacklustre due to the deficiencies of diet and hygiene. A few romping curls scattered the foreheads of the easy-going ladies of the Restoration period and before, but while working women covered their heads for protection against the sun in the fields or against grime in the cities, the smart exchanged the wimple for the wig. The nineteenth century entered with its neo-classical dress ideas and so with the elaborately piled, very seductive long hair associated with the records of the classical world from which the ladies drew their inspiration.

A bas-relief of Cleopatra which points up the importance and erotic mysticism of hair and head-dressing when clothes are both very revealing and very explicit. Naked bodies were two a penny in Ancient Egypt but the elaborate coiffure was quite another turn-on, denoting as it did rank and privilege. This is a pre-couture image of the dress of power.

49

Hair at its most ridiculous (above left): verminous, riddled with lice, evil-smelling, coated in a disgusting mixture of flour, chalk and pomade. No wonder there was a French Revolution. The excesses of the late eighteenth century effectively killed off elaborate hairdressing, or at any rate hair which symbolised such a degree of leisure and money, for 150 years, and Victorian ladies had pretty ringlets and calm chignons to supplant the tousled curls of the raffish Regency aunts. It was not until the 1950s that the cult of the beehive hair-do, not expected to last quite as long as that of a French aristocrat (two months) but still to be lacquered into place for two weeks, revived the untouchable crown (above right). Most of the 1950s hair looked and felt like scouring pads. The smell was less daunting than in the eighteenth century, though – and somewhat less false hair was needed.

The 1920s re-imposed the wimple in the shape of the cloche hat as all girls sought to be good chaps, but the depressed 'thirties revived hair as a goddess symbol and the more unlikely its blonditude, the more exciting and reverenced it was. The coming of peroxide proved what many wealthy Mediterranean ladies had believed for centuries as they purchased the plaits of conquered races from the frozen north: gentlemen prefer blondes. Dark hair has many mysterious associations, but quite frequently they are with evil or alarm. To be worshipped, the goddesses even on the screen had to have performed – no, not a feat of acting, that did not count at all – but a feat of transmogrification worthy of a Delphic priestess. No wonder the film stars were so cautious at revealing their beauty hints. Mystery must still be there and anyway, on a practical note, mixing up the solutions in those experimental days was not the easy thing it is now – who wanted a fan club of Woolworth clerks left with either

50

no hair or an unhappy shade of green?

Hair became an area for attention during World War II, partly because the women of the world were once again closeting their locks in snoods and turbans as they went about their masculinised lives. The neatly rolled bun of the ATS, the fraught chignon of the WRAF as she pushed little model airplanes towards inevitable doom – oh for a twenty-four hours leave, the uniform cap discarded, the hairnet ripped off, the total return of the woman under the uniform. The war helped in a technical sense, too: many of the products which have served to improve, beautify, thicken, curl, straighten or colour hair to an ultimate beauty are spin-offs from scientific research with more deadly initial purpose.

By the mid-1970s hair transplants had become as popular for balding males as cosmetic surgery had for women, and were just as subject to cowboy practitioners.

Since this is a book about the erogenous zones thrown up deliberately by dress, those zones enhanced by make-up or by the obvious use of jewellery to form a point of interest are not of central importance. Nor is the cultural and erotic significance of body hair, but it is interesting that the plucking out of bodily hair was the only physical transformation practised by the ancient Greeks, who viewed the body as a hallowed temple and were emulated by the

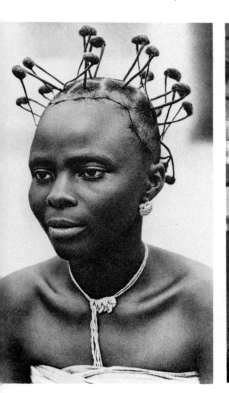

Far left: Real hair, as opposed to a wig, used to denote status and origin. The creativity and ingenuity of ritual hairdressing, while springing spontaneously in some cultures, was adapted to great purpose by others, usually the conquering races.

Left: Another ritual hair-do, that of the 1970s punks, when young people spiked up their hair, using a well-known contraceptive gel to get the right effect. The movement was in fact pacific, and with their knees and ankles chained together they offered easy prey to the aggressive gangs. It is interesting to make a comparison between the effeminacy of punks – which is the girl in this picture? - and the sexual signals worn by girls which show them apparently liberated but which include one element, such as platform shoes, which makes capture not only possible but probable.

Romans. By all accounts it was a process even more painful, since applied to parts more tender, than modern-day depilation, in which Western culture requires the removal of all but the pubic hair on the female. Ironically, Latin countries go furry still, male and female. The other culture in which the systematic removal of body hair was and still is practised in Japan.

The neck, shoulders, arms and hands

Understandably, the upper part of the body plays a proportionately more important part in erogenous dressing when the lower part is covered up, though it has already been noted that the very obvious display of flesh in one area can lead quickly to satiety and induce a yearning to see what is not on show. Thus at the high point of hypocrisy in dress, the mid-Victorian age, very respectable women went about in, and indeed were commanded to appear at Court in, décolletages which we would consider extremely risqué, while the mention of legs was unpardonable and the sight of an ankle deeply moving.

The décolletage did engender excitement in both wearer and viewer, though. A young lady of that time described the frisson of going to the theatre for the first night of an opera by Offenbach, and how hard it was to work out which was the more stimulating – the music, or the sensation of being half-naked in close proximity to a male. For the male, there was the intense excitement of being able to breathe on to – or better, down on to – plump white shoulders with apparent propriety, coupled with the teasing notion that if he could make his fair companion laugh, the whole creation might slip off.

The Victorian appreciation of shoulders was a far cry from that of the peasant culture of centuries, which had favoured an off-the-shoulder blouse above workaday clothes as a lure to suitors interested in a lusty, strong body promising plenty of hard work in the fields and numerous progeny. It was also a far cry from the revival of the wide-necked long dress, fastened with an innocent draw-string, which suddenly appeared on the streets with the 1960s upsurge in do-it-yourself and in societies pledged to protect our planet. As with blue jeans, the revival of a quasi-peasant or working style owed a lot more to pure fashion than had its originals.

Just where to place the strapless dress as an indicator of erogenous zones is hard. Anything so blatant, in many cases so unflattering (bulges or bones popping out of a corsage which needed to be skin-tight to stay put) immediately provoked the desire to see what was under the bits that covered the rest of the body. Since it was those portions which were currently on display in day clothes,

The French designer, Jacques Fath, was famous for his sexy dresses. In this, from one of his last collections in the 1950s, he uses the classic message of black and white, of sleek and full, to re-introduce the allure of the shoulder. Popping up from so elongated a stem, and emerging from ruffles of pristine organdie petals, a woman looks just like a flower – one to be plucked.

though, it could be said that the appearance of the strapless dress in the 1950s merely provided women with an alternative of revelation, and men with a wider option of personal preference to admire. The strapless dress had a brief revival in 1981, most notably when worn by Lady Diana Spencer (now HRH the Princess of Wales) on her first appearance in public with her fiancé. The Princess caused a furore by having to hold up the front of her dress to climb out of her car and then tripping on the long hem as she attempted to negotiate a vast flight of stairs from the top of which the cameras of the world were observing her.

In sophisticated societies the glimpse of the well-turned arm, veiled in translucent fabrics and terminating in a tiny wrist, has always been exciting. That the handsome strong arm and delicate wrist and hand might mete out punishment as well as a caress is well documented in studies of erotic stimulation, and the bliss of being whipped by so sweet a limb features in much erotic literature. On the whole, the hand is viewed as an erogenous zone more when it is covered, for once again there is the implication of intimacy in its disclosure: the drawing-off of gloves is a very calculated gesture. The first item removed by the striptease artist is her glove, the first intimation of familiarity is the touch of the bare hand. To strip off, to peel off, your gloves has a significant message: let's get down to business, let's know one another better. This is why gloves are an integral part of all the most formal dress – the Authority which such dress represents has no wish to get to know anyone better except on its own terms. In modern times the great glove revival was brought about by Jackie Kennedy, who in her all-American, prim, governessy little outfits had hopeful souls yearning to find out if she really was as

Very long gloves with fur at the top. Not a very subtle message this – or is it? Long gloves, particularly with a hirsute trim, are normally considered symbols of feminity, but in this case the gloves are velvet, baggy and deliberately wrinkled. So although they certainly draw attention to the arms, they make them look novelly erotic by suggesting the long-booted legs of a man.

The long 'swan' neck has been regarded as an attribute of beauty for many centuries and in many cultures. Primitive tribes (far left) stretch their necks with rings to what seem impossible proportions – where do the extra bones come from? You feel that if she took the rings off her head must collapse. The 'civilised' version of the ringed neck (left) was revived by Queen Alexandra, accentuated by her daughter-in-law, Queen Mary, and turned into high fashion by yet another Princess of Wales in 1981. The dog-collar in the Western world is often associated with a certain stiff-neckedness which goes well with royalty, clergy and the more stuffy sort of military man, but here is proof that it can be sexy if taken to extreme heights, and not just used to cover wrinkles.

goody-goody as she looked – the implication being that she was not, just playing a delicious game.

The rediscovery of the neck and wrist in modern fashion must be attributed to Cristobal Balenciaga, probably the greatest tailor and architect of dress ever. Balenciaga horrified the fashion pundits by cutting his severest tailleurs not flat or to the figure, but curved most subtly away from the back of the neck and the collar bone so that the head stood up like a flower on a stalk from a neat shell of gabardine, probably black. After the initial reaction that he simply did not know how to make anything fit, the brilliance and innovation of his style was recognised, and when he then sliced off his sleeves to bracelet length, thus revealing for the first time (by day) the wrist bone, the audience did not say that the models looked like schoolboys in outgrown uniforms, but raved at a new erogenous zone.

The stomach, thighs and pudenda

Modern fashionable society is dedicated to the abolition of the stomach, and now that fitness by bodily exercise and the self-mortification of dieting has taken over from panti-girdles and all-in-one corselets, the pursuit of flatness is even more rigorous. The rounded tummy, so admired and worshipped in married women by mankind through all but a few starchy periods, is again out of favour.

55

This Indian carving from the second century AD, by its use of jewellery as dress, provides an analogy with body painting, tattooing and tribal incisions (see page 132). Here, with the exception of the ear-lobes which are mutilated to accommodate substantial gold plugs, the decoration is reversible – though possibly only with a hack-saw. The woman wears an interesting and elegant collar which can also be found on Egyptian references, one upper-arm bracelet and below it on both arms bracelets right up the forearms. Her 'skirt' is an embroidered belt and to finish off the ensemble she wears very wide ankle-bangles which must have made a delicious jingle when she walked. Her nipples are painted but her pubic area has not been made up, though it has been shaved and is explicitly shown by her costume.

Interestingly, the stomach has been repressed in Western fashion only during the reign of, or predominant influence of, women. Thus the Elizabethans constructed rigid cages stretching pointedly down to the pudenda, suppressing the true outline of the natural female figure from armpit to floor. Things went very tight again when Queen Anne was on the throne. A rigid, long, narrow body was once again admired, and once again it was the intricate fastenings of lacings and bows which provided the stimulus for the male to discover what enchantments lay beneath.

56

The thighs have never been emphasised by fashion; indeed, a lot of effort has gone into the work of designers to prove that they do not exist except in the imagination of the male. There, they certainly do exist: all the most ancient fertility symbols from every culture show figurines of females with quite astonishingly developed thighs and buttocks.

The fortunate advent of denim jeans for everyone from granny to toddler provided the perfect excuse for fashion to start working on what had always been working gear. Designers discovered that male and female may want to wear the same clothes, i.e. T-shirt and jeans, but that they are not, nor do they want to be, the same shape. A great many women welcomed the jeans boom because they were mostly made in the first instance for men and so provided a much roomier waist-size in proportion to hip-size, which suited older women or women determined upon comfort very well. It is the great division between cheap and expensive clothes that the former are always cut, for Western consumption, with an eye to the pear-shaped, although the French have always understood the fact that a woman able to afford something pricey is likely to be older, and therefore to have a thicker waist and leaner flanks, than her fertile daughter.

Women in trousers have always presented an interesting challenge to certain men. When the great trouser-suit revolution happened in the 1950s, and after the initial spate of ritual chuckings-out from restaurants of ladies thus clad had subsided, it was clear that a new era for stomach, thighs and pudenda was about to start – for both sexes. For as women wore ever tighter trousers, lengthening their legs with high heels, competing in fact for the masculine phallic image, so too did men. Trousers started to outline every curve of the physique and where they creased, the crease-lines served only to point to the formerly forbidden pubic area. As they shrank and shrank – no longer a sign of poverty and overwashed clothes but the ultimate in sexual indication for modern times – so the lower half of the torso was revealed. Revealed, not guessed at. The symbol of this fashion, because he is portraying an 'ordinary' character as opposed to being a pop star trying deliberately by dress to excite his fans, could be seen to be John Travolta playing a dance-crazed yob in the 1977 movie, *Saturday Night Fever*.

3 THE PEACOCK'S TAIL

'In his bath he is a man, full of magic potentialities. Dressed, the glamour has gone. He is Mr Nobody. Dull in colour, unimaginative in cut, distinguished from the dress of his neighbours in no particular, his clothes might be a prison uniform. Indeed that is precisely what they are, for his spirit is in gaol . . . Rich men, poor men, labourers, intellectuals, bankers, barrow boys, old men, young men, all today dress like robots. There is a terrible cancelling out in their attire, a neuter quality which can only be described as an emasculation.' (Pearl Binder: *The Peacock's Tail*, 1958.)

Twenty-five years later things are not quite so gloomy. Most men have freed themselves in the same way as have women from the diktat of fashion into dressing to suit the way that they feel at a particular moment. It is significant that in May 1981 the popularly priced Hepworth group of shops, which provides the apers of the mighty with an elegance at a fraction the price of Savile Row and with the incalculable authority of a Royal Dressmaker name, Hardy Amies, to bolster the sense of accurate dressing so crucial in this area of menswear, reported trading losses. These they put down to the decline in demand for formal suits and for made-to-measure clothes, which are an indication of forethought and thus formality.

All this at a time of world-wide economic recession. Now, those who seek to tie dress to the Society which wears it – and after all the great Carlyle pointed out that man's earthly interests are all hooked and buttoned together and held up by clothes – would have estimated the formal, even the three-piece suit to be the obvious dress for men seeking employment at a time when labour was in too plentiful supply. But why on earth should the three-piece formal suit be a symbol of hard times? Because it is, or rather was, the only dress of power. It is the dress of old men who prefer to mask their bodies and have the cheque-books to impose their will on generations of the poor. It is the dress, if you like, of jealousy; it has, as Miss Binder says, a neuter quality which can only be described as an emasculation.

Since for so many years power and wealth have been equated with age, and age with a waning virility, it is not hard to come to the conclusion that the ruling party in socio-economic terms took their revenge on handsome, prancing young men who now had to go out to work, by concealing their natural masculine beauty with the figure-demolishing suit. Women, pulled as always between the seduction of the truly splendid man and the ever-practical need for safety and support in financial terms, learned to recognise quickly that this dress, however dull, betokened riches, and thus had a sensual quality all its own. The sexiness of any indication of influence and money should never be underestimated. You only have to glance at the pictures on the society pages showing who is with whom now, or through the history books to see who was with whom, to recognise the power factor; kings, princes and cardinals were not always in first youth, many were given to bad looks (the Hapsburg jaw, for example) or some very nasty habits, but they exuded power. Thus they were free to cloak themselves and their physical shortcomings in panoply, while those with their way still to make had to hope for the best with a neat turn of calf or a borrowed plumage style.

REX.   LUDOVICUS   LUDOVICUS REX

''LUDOVICUS REX.'
From "Paris Sketches."

Unlike modern cricketers and other sportsmen, some early examples of garb for the sport of war provide no codpiece. This early Roman statue (above) shows a hero in a most exposed position. His signal is that of the conqueror, not only in battle but as a virile progenitor. He is wearing a very sharp lapelled suit, and the rolled-up sleeves which form a pad were copied centuries later in middle European uniforms to give a manly breadth to the shoulders of the troops.

John Leech's wicked cartoon, 'Clothes Maketh Man' (left). Based on the famous picture of Louis XIV by Hyacinthe Rigaud, it shows the Sun King in a rather less than shining light.

Precisely the same rules apply today. The presidents of huge corporations, the new princes of society, tend to be ripe in years and wisdom and not all that slim around the waist. The suit, which was born truly of the Industrial Revolution since it was the chosen garb of the new mercantile aristocracy and was made possible to the mass by the technical fruits of their labours (suits were first made on the machines used to furnish the uniforms for the American Civil War), remains their safest shell. That thickening torso is as hidden as under a toga in imperial purple. Around the prince revolve his chosen courtiers. He favours grey? Suddenly, grey is very in. His breakfast meetings require all executives freshly blow-dried and pin-striped, and the number of vents in the back, or the lack of them, can decide promotion or relegation. They present themselves thus. Indeed for the sharp-eyed it is one of the most amusing sights in terms of social commentary to observe the man of power in his drab cloth which hides the sagging flesh surrounded by his clones, who cannot wait to seize the power from him and who to do so are content to wrap their beautiful biceps under an eight-ounce worsted twist from Brooks Brothers. The boss, of course, is London-tailored in a Reid and Taylor specially woven something or other, possibly containing hairs of the tail of the last Derby winner; but that takes a bit of saving up for.

Where Hepworths got it wrong was in not recognising that while the clones of traditional power dressing are still very much with us, especially in America or Japan (that industrial revolution again), there now exists an urgent and overtly expressed need for men to be their own selves. Just as a woman will wear blue jeans and no make-up one day, and then appear in a Zandra Rhodes extravaganza for the evening, or conversely dress for her lover or her business lunch in the highest heels and the nattiest hat, and then slop into a loose housecoat and mules; just as she may spend three times as much on her 'private' clothes, her underwear and her leisure things, as she does on mundane uniform demanded by her career life, so too has the man now come to balance the facets of his life and to feel free at last to express his feelings in clothes.

Bulwer Lytton deplored the effect of commerce upon gaiety, in dress as in much else, in 1838; and 'In their double anxiety to obey a given ethical code and to get on in profitable business the typical men of the new age over-looked some of the other possibilities of life,' wrote G. M. Trevelyan, commenting on the period shortly to engulf Victorian England and to change it from a pastoral agricultural society with a confident aristocracy who could not care a fig what their neighbours thought of their clothes, into a rich, industrialised urban hell. The men went into mourning, and the women went into impossible extravagances of dress to compensate.

Today, the really often extraordinary clothes worn by very ordinary men when they are not on duty is an indication of the changes in Society and in what is now considered erotic in dress.

Erotic dress for men follows much the same pattern of areas as does that for women. The difference is that while the erogenous zones of women seem to be indefinitely extendable, given a degree of subtlety and determination, those of men are both fewer and are more consistently exploited; ever since man began to adorn himself the same polarisations of appeal can be noted. On the one hand is the robe of power which conceals, and on the other is the sheer animal magnetism of a superb body. Both in their way represent the crucial sexual elements needed to attract the female, those of provider (hunter) and sire. I have not forgotten the element of pleasure and sensual excitement, for that too is implicit within these two quite narrow parabolas. For while the imagination and libido of men matches the cunning of women in stimulating it, being as I have said almost infinite, men, perhaps because they have never (or not until very recently) had to compete too much, play under a tighter, simpler set of rules in the game of dress. And women on the whole are satisfied with these narrower options. Of course if he is both beautiful and very rich – well, someday my prince will come, but mainly it turns out to be men who are the dreamers.

The panoply of power, 1982 – on the left are the Chairmen of the five major British clearing banks. Since the Industrial Revolution, the men who hire and fire have dictated the essential outlines of clothing; they are drab, comfortable, but above all they allow younger men who might threaten the boss's position no chance to show off their charms to the women if they want to get on in life. The young, however, can always make a joke out of dress. The teenagers on the right have taken the Chairman's suit, shirt and tie and done monstrous things with it. It's a stab at the Establishment, an expression of individuality, but they will never make the Board. They probably don't want to.

61

Not only do men have fewer erogenous zones than women and exploit them more predictably, but they also seem to be very badly informed as to what they are, or at any rate how preferences have changed among the newly choosy mates of their acquaintance. In a survey taken by the London *Sunday Times* in the late 1970s the physical attributes which men imagined were most desirable to women read as follows in order of preference: muscular chest and shoulders; muscular arms; penis; tallness; flat stomach; slimness; hair (texture not length); buttocks; eyes; long legs; neck.

Let us consider these beliefs, for they have much to answer for in terms of male fashion. By the way, for slimness I would substitute no paunch as being what men think we want. Men are seldom heavy on the thighs. It all adds up to the classic concept of the male body representing in toto the phallus. Work it out: big, broad shoulders, developed muscular arms, in short the rounded powerful testicles on the shaft of a slim, tall body. Elsewhere I shall be examining this concept in more detail since it is now mostly lodged in the clothes of sport – the matador and the American footballer – as it was in uniforms before. As the fighting has got less hand to hand, the physical aspect of fighting gear has switched to another sort of sexual turn-on; that of the scented danger, the smooth, low-profile. Is he or isn't he with the SAS?

For now, we should move on to what physical attributes women apparently require to find the male attractive. These are listed, again in the *Sunday Times* survey, in this order: buttocks (usually described by women as small and sexy); slimness; flat stomach; eyes; long legs; tallness; hair; neck; penis; muscular chest and shoulders; muscular arms. This adds up to a very different picture of the erogenously zoned man, almost a reverse of how he sees himself, in fact. No nasty aggressive bulges, no great penis to threaten damage to that most private area, bland, pretty, above all when he is lying on top of you. For the most startling statistic which could be deduced from the female response to the survey is that British women on the whole get

In the primitive cultures of the Far East, a man will use a piece of wood as an exaggerated representation of his penis, or wrap it in yards of cotton to an elaborate pattern, and finish up with a phallic weapon two feet long. Such decorations sometimes include grass tufts on the end which are not merely decorative or protective but also symbolise the spouting sperm. To prevent this precious bundle from catching in the undergrowth, the penis is then held up by a string or leather belt against the stomach. The testicles remain bare. Drawing attention to your virile member has many other fashionable references: the Peguans of South Burma, for example, wore little jewelled bells, similar to those on women's stepping chains, which tinkled as they went about. Greek drama is filled with characters whose sole costume was an enormous false phallus. Slip-over embellishments to supplement an unsatisfactory natural proportion can today be bought at all good sex shops.

62

The anonymous menace of the hooded executioner. In this case the menace is real, for these are IRA gunmen on the streets of Belfast. But that they have a following is clear from the youngsters pressing round them; heroes come in all guises. At the leisured and sophisticated end of dress, this look is associated with fetishism.

their sex from the front. It is a long-standing joke that the women of these islands spend their coital lives gazing at the ceiling but what with emancipation and all that they have now got round to the fact that if they are going to be laid that way, then flat, small sexy buttocks are nice to fondle, a big stomach requires an altogether different position for comfortable accommodation, eyes cannot lie and even the hardest of females hopes to see 'babies in his eyes' (i.e. Cupid, the baby god of love, alive in his pupils), even for a minute. The accent on both the hair and neck completes this supposition, since it is undoubtedly the back of the neck and the hair above the back of the neck which women mean. These are far best savoured from the missionary position, so scorned by the ancients and so loved by the guilt-ridden Christians.

Another point to be examined before we move on to dress our alternative man is the high rating of the penis in the men's view compared to the women's. As many men, it seems, worry and fuss about the size of their member as do women over the size of their breasts. One of the greatest blessings of the disintegration of accepted fashion in beauty as in many other areas must be to make intelligent people realise that in any area where you have a choice, it should be each to his choice. That it comes low in the survey of attributes required by women should support this theory.

The fashion for the man chosen by the women is . . . but you've guessed – the three-piece suit. Safe, avuncular, cuddly and protective. The replete man, not the hungry man in his blouson. Reliable, you know, not a wham, bam, thank you ma'am type. No waking up with your head in the pillow and wondering where am I or more pertinently where is *he*? It's the Rolls purring at the door, the worry taken that your dress might have to brush the pavement, the hovering waiters, the unmolested return home; it's the potence of impotence, if you like, and it lurks in the primary pin-stripe.

The Lord Lieutenant of the county, Majesty's representative in an area of the realm, taking precedence over all save when Majesty itself is present, looks distinctly uncomfortable, but then so do all the formally suited men around him. His collar may be higher, his tunic and trousers tighter, he may have to keep in mind the necessity of not stepping backwards too fast and gouging an ankle with his heel, he certainly has to remember not to clout anyone with his sword.

But my, what a handsome figure he cuts. Every man is boiled to lobster shade, longing to be free of his jacket, since lightweight suitings for summer have yet to reach the British provinces, and what is more it is possible that anyone wearing them, at any rate at a county occasion, might just be considered something of a bounder, trying to vault the hedges imposed by Authority.

Power resides not only in the mind of the wielder but in the mind of the public, and what the public wants is continuity, which is why it is such a mistake for rulers to try to be fashionable nowadays. However paunchy, bespectacled, bow-legged or generally unlikely the four heralds for the Investiture of Prince Charles as Prince of Wales in 1969 might look to the cynic or to the fashion critic, they indubitably got away with it on the day because the symbolism of their clothes outweighed their physical properties. In medieval times, heralds were chosen from the ranks of the younger nobility for their grace and bearing and were likely to be aged about twelve, so they were able to dodge out of the way if the meeting they were heralding looked like turning into a hassle. Now that the office is purely ceremonial, the effect created by the holders of these offices is one of solid tradition.

ÆSTHETICS.—Drawn by GEORGE DU MAURIER.
(*Scene—A London Drawing-Room after Dinner.*)

VAN TROMP:—"Oh, Sir Charles! modern English male attire is *too* hideous! Just look round.....there are only two decently dressed men in the room!"
CHARLES:—"Indeed; and which are *they*, may I ask?"
VAN TROMP:—"Well—I don't know *who* they are, exactly—but just now one of them seems to be offering the other a cup of tea!"

The boringness of male clothes which was imposed during the Victorian era is remarked by the artist George du Maurier in this 1889 cartoon, in which the American lady visitor identifies as the only two men in the room with sartorial pulling-power the footman and the bishop, the former in a very natty outfit which shows his handsome figure in Regency style, the latter exuding power and authority.

But uniform imposes quite another discipline, both on wearer and on viewer. While the concept of discomfort in dress is anathema to a large section of the public, and particularly now to women as they try out not just men's jobs and status but their clothes too, there remains an acceptability of discomfort in menswear which is in fact growing as women refuse the corseting of bondage.

While the gear of real war is drab and unindividual, that reserved for State occasions is filled with the resonance of prestige, power, Authority, standards of yore not nibbled at by yobs in blue jeans, in fact a sense of superiority because uniform of such state is now so rare that it implies an intimacy on a par with a silk-lined couture dress. You have to belong, and to understand what you are wearing.

State uniform thus remains very exciting for the observer, and intrinsically exciting for the wearer. The fact is that it is uncomfortable, that it does demand sacrifice to the demands of Authority or Society, to shore up the confidence of one or the other. I doubt that the recruiting sergeant gets far from his drab desk these days in fact, but what a job is done for him by the advertisements of the hardware anyone in the services will control. Thus the garb of heroes in this area has moved from man to machine.

A sympathetic onlooker might feel that there was a cause for the imposition of sumptuary laws by rulers, temporal or spiritual, against the anachronism of much menswear. In the case of uniform, I doubt that they would be welcomed. There is no doubt how waist-conscious men have always been, and also how addicted to high, tight bindings at the neck, whether by gilded military collar, cravat, or swan-necked armour. Curiously, this tight binding at the neck is something which has appealed to young women in the early 1980s who have adopted the Swashbuckling style. It also appealed to Madame de Pompadour; but while for men the attraction of being held in firmly seems to exist all over, from dress uniform to Dr Jaeger's reform suits (just like Chairman Mao's), the modern girls who look romantic and piratical hit smack between Madame, with all her frills and laces and tight décolletage and *then* the tight bow at the neck, and the sloppy Byron romantic dress with *then* the tight masculine cravat above almost an equally bare expanse of flesh. Everywhere else, they are free.

Corsets for men pose many more questions than they do for women and arise from three major sources. The first is the desire for a slender figure, always thought aristocratic. To be stout might be all right for an alderman or a tradesman, who depended on bulk and were subject to limited dress, but the aristocrat was always slim – to show that he could afford to eat when he chose – and the bulk, essential to his status, was imposed by his dress.

Charles Dana Gibson, creator of the Gibson Girl, obviously had a sense of humour. Poking fun at Reformed Dress and the efforts of women to adopt portions of men's clothing, in 1889 he got away with a cartoon for *Life*, very much a man's magazine, which showed men in décolleté evening tops based on the correct tail-coat but without sleeves and dipping at the back to show the requisite amount of Edwardian spine. The effect is blurred now because transvestitism is becoming commonplace in public, but on its publication it must have been quite something. One wonders how many men cut it out and locked it away to dream about.

WHY NOT?

Slenderness also presupposed, and to an extent still does, youthfulness, which has been equated with virility. Thus corseting, and the general desire for tight-fitting dress by men, has an enormous content of vanity. When men's vanity was at its height – and it has hardly ever diminished until the nineteenth century – there was no discomfort that men would not suffer. If their breeches were loose enough to bend down in, they sent them back to the tailor. 'The Cherrypickers don't dance,' a moustachioed young blood informed his hostess, who was in quest at an Edwardian party of partners for the gels. The reason that they did not dance was that they practically could not move from the lounging position, certainly not sit down or cavort, without splitting their trousers.

Unlike their louche predecessors, notably of the fourteenth and very early nineteenth centuries, their material masculine parts were discreetly covered. Their legs and thighs, however, even when booted, were much in evidence.

Another aspect of eroticism in men mysteriously unmentioned either in the *Sunday Times* survey or anywhere else that I can find is the erotic appeal of stance and deportment. I admit that this in itself hardly qualifies under erotic dress, but then deportment is so often determined by dress. Dancers sway in lovely costumes, so do men strut in peacock finery. Much of that is now reserved in the case of men to private lives, where anything goes, and in public to national (the great excuse for fancy) dress.

While bulk in men's dress has always symbolised Authority, the slim figure, with its associations of youth and vitality and above all of aristocratic breeding – no need to gorge and gobble because you know where the next meal is coming from – has always been sought after. The overstuffed fellow on the left of this 1829 cartoon thinks it can be done by tailoring. Smarty-boots on the right is pointing out that his clothes are cut on the 'Anatomical principal'.

If men walk tall and proud in uniform, so do they in, say, the kilt, which retains just as much mystery as any skirt of the time before underwear for women. Skirts for men – which developed after all from just another arrangement of one piece of cloth (as did drawers, which were more practical for certain forms of masculine life) – have always symbolised a certain pioneering and aggressive spirit. Interestingly, the two greatest examples of skirted pioneers, the Scots and the Romans, come from opposite ends of the original areas of civilisation. While the brutish Scandinavians and Huns were getting themselves together into the dress of the demolished or the demolisher – serf or destroyer in their practical trousers – the Romans and the Scots were fast, mobile survivors, conquerors of empires. On a man, the skirt is the dress of sleeping rough, of mobility, of taking what he wants, when he wants. No wonder it gives them such a cocky walk, though now more men are learning to strut again, as women become more demanding and choosey.

The garb of heroes

> 'Leap thou, attire and all,
> Through proof of harness to my heart, and there,
> Ride on the pants triumphing.'
> > (Shakespeare: *Antony and Cleopatra*.)

I must say that I have always thought that that scene was infinitely more sexually prepossessing than the terse, typical Brit note penned by the first Duchess of Marlborough to record that her husband, a great little man, had got back from Malplaquet or wherever without having been blown to bits and had not even waited to take off his boots before leaping into bed with her. Cold-blooded observers of military dress might point out that it was all very well for Mark Antony, even in full Roman armour, to comply with his mistress's wishes (Rome had refused to acknowledge their marriage in 37 BC) but for the future Duke the garb of the time would have necessitated a good deal of undressing. Also, while Mark Antony, naked beneath his kilt, was notoriously handsome – 'Of fine physique, and with a constitution which excesses and hardships alike failed to ruin,' states the *Oxford Classical Dictionary* primly – no records remain to tell us about the undressed side of John Churchill. With a full, red lower lip and those slightly pop eyes of the beauties favoured by Charles II, he looks sexy enough in full fig though.

What both stories illustrate is the lusty power of martial glory implied through dress. Of course the ageing (well, she was thirty-

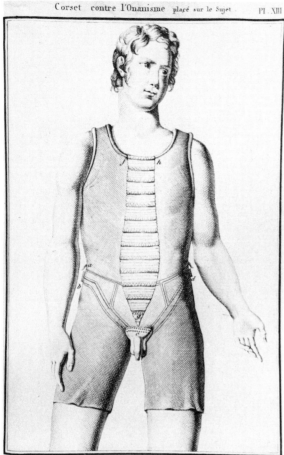

Will the French never give up on fashion? This outfit (left) is designed to prevent masturbation and for chic it must be said that it beats sewing up the lad's trouser-pockets any time. This 'orthopaedic' garment is dated around 1815 when one might have thought that Europe had other matters on its mind; and that the model ought to be past such childish pranks. The message, of course, is that this so-called preventive outfit is far more erotic than ordinary underwear — look at all those carefully top-stitched seams leading to the penis.

And now we know. Something does go on underneath the kilt, at any rate when it is swirling in public beneath the Royal gaze of Princess Margaret (below); in this case it was mini-briefs. These four soldiers are performing the Sword Dance at a fashion spectacular in Munich in 1981. It has not been established whether on leaving barracks on normal duty they are still expected by their colonel to walk over a mirror, but the cocky swirl of the kilt, and the graceful movements of a dance which both in costume and intent goes back a long, long way, illustrate the excitement of folkloric rituals.

The Emperor Augustus, prime exponent of the public relations picture, or rather depiction. In order to placate his subject provinces he had himself shown in dress which would appeal to and not offend local opinion, a case of Caesar rendering unto sulky and possibly rebellious areas of the Empire the things that were theirs. In Rome he could afford to be shown in full classic glory, as here – kilted but carrying an extra plaid, and wearing superb, figure-forming armour with religious symbols. Compare the widening of the shoulders by rolled sleeves and epaulettes with the early Roman figure shown on page 59. He is bare-footed, again a suggestion of greatness; his feet would never need to touch down.

nine) Cleopatra saw Mark Antony as a political pawn in her survival game. Hoary veteran as she was, determined as she must have been even at that moment to dump Antony as a loser, to betray him at Actium and to bury herself in further gallons of asses' milk in order to seduce a third great conqueror, Octavian, yet Shakespeare allows her the dignity of real sexual desire. This splendid man, this incredibly virile figure – he was fifty-two – this encapsulation of power, sex, beauty and the dangers he had risked by siding with her just as she (he thought) had gambled by siding with him in the battle for power in Rome, was an incomparable turn-on. Looming in her tent door, huge, boyish, adoring, entranced by the subtle veils which masked the fact that she was not eighteen, deluded by perfumes and soft fans into seeing her not as the snake that she was (what an apposite death) but as the ideal of eternal feminity, Antony counted the world well lost. She is anxious. Has he been seduced while he has been away in Rome, has another woman won him from her? But no, he smiles and laughs as he possesses her again and so she knows that she is not just a need, she is a must, for him.

Did the first Duchess of Marlborough have such heroic thoughts in mind when she commissioned the Column of Victory at Blenheim Palace, Oxfordshire, 134 feet high and topped with a representation

70

Macho man. Charles V of Germany and Spain, painted by Titian in clothes which show the inverted phallus shape at its most glorious; the head is insignificant, the shoulders are huge and rounded, the waist is very narrow, as are the thighs in tight drawers, and the legs and feet are not accentuated. Lest the message be too subtle, he wears the statutory codpiece to signal not just power but virility.

of her husband in Roman armour, a theme which is taken up again in Rysbrack's monument in the family chapel? It could be argued that the choice of dress for both memorials reflects nothing more than the current taste for being portrayed in classical gear for the practical reason that it would not date. The duke died in 1722, and in 1711 Addison had remarked in his series of essays for *The Spectator* that 'Great masters in painting never care for drawing people in the fashion; as very well knowing that the head-dress, or periwig, that now prevails, and gives grace to their portraitures at present will make a very odd figure, and perhaps looks monstrous in the eyes of posterity. For this reason they often represent an illustrious person in a Roman habit, or in some other dress that never varies.' The classical concept had been indeed given regal blessing, for the statue of the ill-fated James II of England (1633–1701) which now stands outside the National Gallery in Trafalgar Square shows him, pensive withal, in the dress of an armed Roman victor. Depending on what it was intended for, though, Roman armour, especially the moulding of the breastplate which reached in a curve right down to the groin in the front, exaggerated to a greater or lesser degree the precise details of the masculine torso it enclosed. Thus for a statue designed for the celebration of victory and benevolence, an arch-propagandist such as

71

When George Washington was depicted in Roman garb by Horatio Greenough (right), the American nation was horrified. Viewed with detachment, it is hardly surprising that a nation devoted to the democratic ideal, which had just broken ties with an Empire, should have rejected the concept of their liberator decked out like a killer Emperor. Aesthetically, it really is a dreadful sculpture because it is far too truthful. If you are going to show your subject as a hero, you have to beef up his torso, adapt his hairstyle and generally turn him into a sexy power-object; a too-realistic casting of a weedy torso does not fit with the public image of the ideal bringer of law, order and justice. Just compare the ersatz Washington with the real thing (far right). Even minus an arm and a leg, the Roman general's magnificent figure exudes power, virility, justice and the protection which is very appealing to women. He has a very steady gaze, too, the sort of look you hope to see on the pilot of your Boeing 747. With those wrinkles around the neck he is not so young, but he is mighty handsome.

the emperor Augustus would be shown with the pectoral muscles insinuated but not stressed, while for an image destined for a more primitive area the fertility aspects of his virile form would be accentuated. That Augustus' manipulation of the media as a propaganda machine was successful might be judged from the fact that he reigned for forty-five years, 31 BC to AD 14, an unprecedented length of power for his date.

But what is fascinating to discover is that in commemorating the Great Duke the artist has used his licence to the extreme in selecting explicit, body-showing armour, which in its way is even more sexy than a naked torso because it is decked in the apparel of power and conquest and yet leaves little to the imagination as to the handsome rippling muscles below. It is therefore a far more clever and stimulating dress for a hero than that attempted by Horatio Greenough, an American sculptor, in a portrayal of George Washington. Seeking the usual channels of datelessness by classical garb, and the chance to make something daring under the guise that the sparse outfit had impeccable antique ancestry, Greenough knocked out a massive seated figure in the capital city, and dressed George W. in what he imagined was a toga.

Where Greenough went wrong – the statue horrified the prim folk and was relegated to the Smithsonian Institute – was that he went too far one way and not far enough in another. His periwigged George Washington reveals a shrimpy torso and appears to be garbed not in the confidence of virile splendour but in a bed sheet. As a work of art it is a dreadful piece which makes a mockery of valiance because its effect is not to show GW as a sempiternal conqueror but as somebody who has just donned hastily whatever was nearest to hand in an emergency and who seems to be pointing the way not to Olympus but to the Fire Exit. Compare this weedy, unerotic, besandalled figure, which nevertheless caused a scandal, with the figure of the real Roman general in the same basic outfit. Of course we do not know what he was doing with his right arm, which has got lopped off over the centuries, but I bet it was not indicating an escape route.

The traditional explanation of the lure of the armed figure has been that it implies to the nesting female a sense of strength to secure a safe territory for herself and her brood. Since practically all wars, animal and human, have been fought on the principle of lebensraum with all its associations of economic self-sufficiency, it follows that any group identifiable by its appropriate garb and armament which suggest such power is liable to prove attractive to the female. It might be worth reminding readers that it is only in recent years, since wars have been fought for (often obscure) political ideologies and not widely comprehensible needs that uniform has been reduced from glory to guilty rags and that woman, with her determination for equality, has found herself no longer a prize, albeit unwilling, of the conqueror but just another victim to be knocked out.

From the earliest, the armed figure has symbolised power and privilege. While the whole of the Roman army was kitted out in a style both ergonomic and terror-inspiring and was thus the perfect illustration of the Republican and democratic principle, its efficiency and its intention to conquer and then to settle the vast areas which fell to it (the farmer/soldier concept, now fashionable in Israel), in other cultures it was normally the individual who starred. Thus the glittering knight in armour was liable to be a king, a prince, a great territorial lord, in fact a hero. The wretched rabble dragged from their ploughs in his fields made do as best they might in everyday clothes and had no more sex appeal than any other boy next door.

It was not until the twentieth century that the common soldier, on at any rate some pay unlike the wretched agricultural labourers

Classical armour as fancy dress: Louis XIV, 'who made the earth tremble and never trembled himself', runs the caption to this unconvincing piece of hagiography. The beady-eyed might be forgiven for wondering if, once the painters had got that weary-lidded look and down-turned mouth to the King's liking, they just went on reproducing it – see the John Leech cartoon on page 59.

starving in their pig-styes, became the cynosure of every Victorian domestic servant's eye. The handsome sergeant vied with the local policeman to gossip with the housemaids and the nursemaids through the area railings of Belgravia. Uniform implies social security. It gives a man that confidence and swagger which females find irresistible. It seems that they always have done. Suetonius, writing the biography of Octavian, he who had refused the advances of Cleopatra and gone on to become Augustus, says that 'his appearance was distinguished and graceful'. This suggests that his manly deportment over-rode his lack of teeth and churchmouse-coloured hair. As I have mentioned earlier in this chapter, the deportment of the male figure has great erotic appeal, once again pinned to that mast of sexual allure, confidence.

Just as the army dress was becoming popularised and less exclusive, and thus only of interest to the mass of humanity, a whole new breed of 'military' looks evolved. They too were bound up with the

74

conquest of territory, and they stem from America. The Americans, with a brand-new sense of advertising euphemistic jargon at their door, called their conquest, their driving to starvation, of the indigenous Red Indians in order to provide homes for right-thinking homesteaders, 'Manifest Destiny'. The executioners of this grisly doom, which brought to the conquered none of the benefits of the Roman judicial and travel facilities, not even central heating, nor any of those of the British Empire with its supreme examples of impartial justice and efficiency in administration, were heroes to their people, too. They wore the dress of the hot, arid West, or they wore the uniform of the US Cavalry. So they, too, were official.

As the clocks chimed in the twentieth century the golden coach of Britain changed back into a pumpkin. Sure, the pumpkin still had wheels – 900 years of unconqueredness lends a certain oil to the machinery, a certain prance to the nags who drag the pomp and circumstance around – but we began to be losers in a big way. Society was corrupt, immoral and hypocritical, rulership a sham of established incompetents, the conditions of our poor a scandal to all other civilised nations, our army deplorably led, the disgraceful exploitation of women and children only just somewhat ameliorated. The wheels finally fell off the pumpkin in 1914 when the innocent seed of all this fatuous dissembly actually was made to believe that it ought to go out and die in disgusting circumstances for no purpose whatever except the ideals inculcated by vaporous and unfaithful parents whose high point of conversation was was it going to be ortolans again for dinner, who committed their children to torturing schools and servants and who simply bred the guts out of them.

But Society, as I point out in a later chapter, will survive come whatever, and so, discovering themselves to be a natural race of losers, the British made it the accepted thing to be good at that. What would Elizabeth I have said? What would her father have said? What would the 900 years of exploiters, pirates, buccaneers, industrialists, East India men, mercenaries, slave-traders, tea-importers, to say nothing of Henry V and Livingstone, have said? Perhaps it would not have been so bad had the good-loser complex not bitten, as fashions always do, from clever, quick-footed trendsetters via Authority and thus eventually deep into the masses.

These thoughts were all in my mind as I watched Bjorn Borg beaten at Wimbledon for the first time in six years by John McEnroe, for I was considering what part is played by beauty and style in the acceptability of heroes, and heroes to me are winners, not losers, on the whole. Since beauty and style are intrinsic to dress you will see where I am leading. By nationality if not by nature inclined to support the loser – thus being the exact opposite of the American dream, where 'nobody talks to the runner-up' – was it because he lost that I found Borg for once quite sublimely attractive and sexy: the drooping, Christ-like head with the oft-auctioned bandeau no more now than a crown of thorns, that extraordinary face which makes him look so like Holman Hunt's insipid interpretation of another great winner/loser in 'The Light of the World', and under the insipidness that amazing strength and endurance, the knowledge that even in defeat there is a certain victory.

So do heroes have to be handsome? Would people be less spiteful about the great Field-Marshal Lord Montgomery of Alamein had he not been short, plain and considered rather common by silly social superiors? Would his mother have accepted him eventually to her love had he been handsome? So, I enquired, would the tennis sets have forgiven John McEnroe his foul behaviour if he were not so ugly and graceless? No one seemed to know. I suspect it would divide the sexes: women prepared to allow a hero who looked like, say, Lew Hoad almost unlimited licence, men much more stern, and men, certainly in Britain, tremendously concerned as to whether the fellow was properly dressed and behaved well and preferably just lost.

I chose tennis for this philosophical ramble into the garb of heroes because it comes closest to the man-to-man gladiatorial contests (in which losing, by the way, was apt to be a big mistake) in that it requires superb physical agility and fitness, the greatest powers of endurance, a knowledge as close as any race-horse trainer's of the speed and tactics of your opponent (who may then fool you by doing the opposite), a mental capacity for intense concentration, and hawk-like hunting eyes for a chance to kill. Moreover, it is a very lonely game. At least in boxing there is direct physical contact, even if it is the other man giving you a bloody nose. In tennis you are alone, actually separated by a taut, high net. Have you never wondered why people jump over it to clasp their opponents' hands? It may be their first physical contact with another of their species for three and a half hours. Footballers can leap in the air and kiss anyone that they fancy, American footballers have frequent periods on the sidelines gossiping, and in rugby everyone is sitting on everyone else half the time anyway. The matador is within inches of his living, breathing opponent. The pop idol has his musicians.

One would think therefore that in tennis, dress would play a crucial part in making the wearer feel good (the eroticism of intimacy) and also appealing to the vast audiences. Yet at what remains the première championships of the world, Wimbledon, the dress is stultifyingly dull to the observer, though filled it seems with inner meaning for its wearer. Just two and a half yards of white is

From the front (at Wimbledon anyway, before which he never shaves), the magnificent tennis-player, Bjorn Borg, looks too Pre-Raphaelite for those whose taste in heroes runs more to the overtly muscular stuff. But viewed from behind, Borg reveals an almost perfect physique: broad, powerful shoulders, a deep chest, a very small waist, tight, high buttocks, strong, slim legs and small feet. Above all, there is no singular distortion of the perfect form because he concentrates on one game; the Greeks always made their finest athletes try many sports in order that the balance of the body should not be upset, and when one looks at certain tennis-players with one forearm like a ham and the other like a shoestring, one can see that the Greek ideal of masculine beauty had a lot going for it. Here on the Centre Court, the hero acknowledges his worshippers.

What Bjorn Borg was given by Nature, American footballers are given via padding. This lethal sport – the average career expectancy of a top-class player is three years, the most likely cause of his retirement a knee injury – attracts docile crowds of thousands into huge stadia where the entertainment rivals the ancient circuses. Music blares in triumph when anyone touches the ball, ravishing maidens in scanty costumes perform a vestal dance between runs (to the fury of the liberationists who, missing the point yet again, think this is exploitation of women) and strange figures appear on plumed horses or leading goats or rams which are patently drugged. In terms of dress, the American footballer is first cousin to the matador: emphasised shoulders, tiny waist, and backside tapering to tightly-laced feet. The head is covered and insignificant.

acceptable in the arena, so it is not surprising to find out from the best known of all sportswear designers, Ted Tinling, that every single player, star or ingenue, has a set of fixations about her clothes and her underclothes which would do justice to a Givenchy private customer. They have their birth signs embroidered in rhinestones on their knickers, and if they're winning they have been known to wear the same dress every day, while close up every garment is a masterpiece of hand-sewn couture which only they and their intimates know about. I have yet to discover whether the male players demand polyester satin linings to their shorts, though I do know that some like them exceptionally tight and some have a predilection for front pockets. But mostly they must rely upon their own God-given body, with very little ergonomically feasible in terms of alteration, for their outward appeal. Quite hard.

It is therefore very interesting to observe that Bjorn Borg happens to possess the almost perfect physique if one is to go by the demands of women as listed in the *Sunday Times* survey or, far more obviously, as indicated by the efforts of Society over the centuries. He is from the back by nature exactly what the costumiers strive for in the outfits of other gladiators. He has height, width where it should be and not where it should not be. He has the hands of an artist and the feet of an aristocrat. He also has a kingly, somewhat aloof bearing. But is it because he is so near to perfect that he seems a trifle dull?

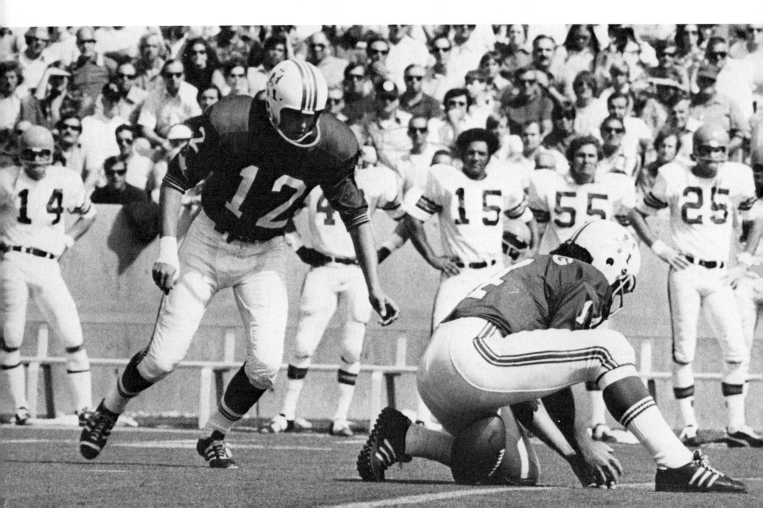

Now take a think about the back view of American footballers and Spanish bullfighters, both of which species are dressed in the classic inverted phallic shape. Big, rounded shoulders, short neck and hair rather insignificant, tapering sharply to a tiny waist, accentuated by a sash, always short-jacketed, skin-tight trousers highlighting small, high, rounded buttocks, slim thighs tapering to small, pointed feet. The American footballer does it with pads and is the ultimate sublimation of the god-hero to the dictates of Authority and Society, a perfectly acceptable fertility symbol, a real turn-on for the watchers. The matador, who has been around longer, is equally padded to enhance his manly form (and offer protection as in football) but because his game is one of real life and death he lards himself with sequins and as much glamour as the gladiator's armour which must equally have glinted on the sandy floor among the blood.

Pop idols now face almost as much physical danger as the matador from their howling mobs and lunatic fans yet at the same time since their act, as with American football, depends to so great an extent on display and provocation which will not actually lead to a fight to the death, not surprisingly stage-heroes have always been most erotically dressed. For many weeks during the early 1980s the British pop record sales charts were topped by a group called Adam and the Ants. Adam Ant (real name Stuart Goddard) is a slim lad with chronic myopia who wears a selection of braided hussars' jackets, or naval uniform of the Nelson era, under highwayman cloaks and with his face painted like a punk Indian chief. The kids adore him, and anybody susceptible to dress must do so too, because he combines a touch of just about everything. Uniform, denoting conquering aspects, big padded shoulders of the hero, romantic swirl of wicked cape, the 'once aboard the lugger and the girl is mine' appeal, and a scent of danger; then he has ducky little trousers and great natural grace of movement (very important, as I have mentioned in the wearing of the kilt, for example). The effect is as if he had borrowed something from every known source of eroticism in dress, but it is clear when you speak to him that it is quite unconscious, quite uncalculated.

D. H. Lawrence is inexplicit about just what Gerald Crich was wearing in the scene in the novel, *Women in Love*, where he forces his terrified mare to face the oncoming express train at the level-crossing gates rather than turn tail and flee, as all her natural horse instincts would advise her to do. Her shrinking flanks are whipped and spurred as Crich makes the female in his mastery defy each and every impulse for safety given by nature to creatures which have no weapons for survival save fleetness of foot. No tusks, no claws, no deadly venom, no quills or horns. On the contrary, a delicious and

79

most tempting morsel for sexual or dinner delights. Pretty women are always described by sexist writers as being 'doe-eyed' or of 'gazelle-like grace' or some equally insipid anthropomorphism and you can easily see why, just as you can see why the first thing men do to women in clothes is to insist on styles which make fleet escape impossible – platform soles go with the vote and the mini.

My guess is that Mr Crich was wearing just ordinary working gear; he needed no special costume to prove the point of his domination of the female, just something as comfortable and ergonomic as the singlet of a truck driver. The erotic implications were there all right, though. This quivering, reluctant, wilful female must be forced to accept the throbbing masculine power of the steam engine, inexorably penetrating her private territory; in the case of the horse, to within feet of her velvet muzzle and sweat-drenched ears. In the case of the human female, between her legs.

The dress of heroism comes in many guises but, most socially significant, in many classes. This explains the reverence which is accorded to working clothes, because working clothes suggest a mastery, either of all Gaul in the case of Roman armour, or of a vast animal in the case of the matador; that sense of conquest once reserved for martial splendour (the end of hand-to-hand combat finished off uniform glamour except that from the past) or for a huge Mack truck covered in phallic horns and throbbing power from every cylinder as it bears down inexorably on huge wheels as the hapless blonde skelters away in her antique Mini. Who is to say that the knights of the road are any less exciting than Crusaders were, as they perch on cab seats twice the height of shire horses, surrounded by Volvo armoured plate and what is more roaring off to do battle in exotic, far-off lands, even if their cause is commerce not the Church?

Why should smarty-pants Texans bother to wear a hat designed to shade the sun from the head of a poor, hard-worked illiterate cowpoke? Because, ma'am, them was gallant fellows, loyal, hardworking and decent, and the conquerors of territory, the homesteaders who produced a safe nest for people yearning to breathe free. Thus does Society select dress whose original function was one of survival, and give it connotations of erotic pride and glamour.

Another hero given in dress in America to the rest of us has been the doctor. The moment that I noticed my dentist in a white, shortsleeved, high-necked gown, with his strong muscly forearms so densely covered with dark fur, I thought – well, what I actually thought was, I hope to God he's not going to tell me that I have to have a filling. But I could quite understand the allure of TV hospital soap operas and of the school of medical light literature for which love among the bedpans has proved a winning formula.

The overtly sexy vehicles of the long-distance truckers are covered with chrome pipes, tubes and bits and pieces which are lovingly polished by their drivers. The allure of the trucker, with just enough time for a tryst but with engine throbbing outside as well as inside, is well documented, particularly in American literature. For Englishwomen, entry to the Common Market brought the chance to enjoy the delights of the singleted and tattooed Italian, French and German master of the mammoth vehicle which was shattering their windows and possibly their drab marriages, as bronzed and muscley forearms braked the brute to a halt to enquire the way to Liverpool.

The cowboy tradition dies hard. In Texas they still wear the ten-gallon hat even if it is to a company meeting to discuss ten-billion-dollar contracts. In the late 1970s the TV series called simply *Dallas* became required viewing for most of the world, and the sexiest man in the show was the through-and-through nasty guy, J.R. Ewing. Played by Larry Hagman, 'JR' epitomises the dreams of many men, being foul to his family and his wife, cheating everyone in sight, reneging on every deal, a terror with women, a terror to men. He always wears a stetson, even with a Savile Row suit, but being a smart guy he often has bird feathers or other decoration around the crown whereas a real cowpoke could have had just a sweat-drenched band of leather.

Richard Chamberlain as Dr Kildare. What that young man did for the medical profession! Even Harley Street is into short sleeves now, at any rate among the furry-forearmed. Does it hurt less if they are sexy?

4 THE SHORT HAUL TO HYPOCRISY

WHEN Anne Askew was burned at the stake in 1546, King Henry VIII apparently instructed that she be carried to her execution in a chair. This he did not from any sense of mercy, to ease the final path to her hideous death, but because his masculine pride was endangered. To the common people, his putting aside of Katherine of Aragon (because she could not give him a son) was acceptable because she came of the hated Spanish stock, and his determination to be rid of Anne Boleyn (who could not give him a son) because she was uppity, improper in her ways and tremendously pretty (always a good basis for common spite) was also acceptable, but that their golden king, their Hal, their once-youthful champion of all that was great and gallant, would allow a delicate woman to be subjected to torture, that would be to destroy for ever the image of good luck, and the fertility which goes with good luck and gallant kingship.

Brutal Henry understood this perfectly well, so that although he allowed Anne Askew to be torn almost in half on the rack in order to extract some evidence against his wife, Anne Boleyn, he knew in his heart that he could not bear to be known to have agreed to this assault upon womanhood. The age of chivalry was not to perish until the arrival of the Puritan regime, when women were to be regarded as the work of the Devil. Harry was still close enough to the Whore of Rome to think that a man of power was a handsome, chivalrous man, too courteous to allow such cruelty to the fair sex. He had, after all, been betrayed by sensual beauty, by the sight of a lovely, presumably fecund girl, which made his own inadequacy so much the worse. He had always been a Ladies' Man, had he not?

82

Rumour has it that the codpiece of this armour belonging to King Henry VIII, which is on display at the Tower of London, continually has to be replaced or re-hinged because it acts as a fetish-touch object just as irresistible as a rock star's shirt. To touch is to imbibe some trace of the power and the glory of the worshipped idol. In the National Air and Space Museum of the Smithsonian Institution in Washington DC they have a tiny sliver of the moon surface which you are invited to touch, in much the same way as pilgrims have worn bare the toes and noses of countless holy effigies in shrines all over the world.

This concept of the eroticism of the dress of virility, of 'a good harvest' whether of grain, corpses in battle, further extensions of your territory or whatever, was not extinguished in Western European dress until the early seventeenth century, but Henry VIII was the last English king to recognise virile overt manliness as a prerequisite of Authority. Elizabeth, his daughter, dressed for power play, and subsequent kings, aldermen, Lord Mayors and associated sycophants of power have opted either for the safe get-out of classical dress or the topical dress of power.

It is a sure sign of alarm in rulers when they start fussing about what the others are wearing. The decline and fall of the Roman

King and God and sacrifice. In 1911, King George V and Queen Mary of England decided at the prodding of politicians to revive the antique custom of actually showing the Prince of Wales to his people. Back in the fourteenth century, the first Prince had been in no position to argue about what to wear, since he had been a baby and held up in his father's shield, but the preposterous dress invented for the luckless David, later so briefly to become Edward VIII, shows the extent to which Authority felt it necessary to make a formal impact with dress. The King, who was to reign during one of the most frightful conflicts in history, the First World War, wears martial garb signifying power, in this case over the seas since he is dressed as an Admiral. The Queen, herself a sacrifice to duty before love, is already the icon, goddess figure of morality and family life.

empire may be dated from the time when the use of silk, a secret process stolen from China by the Church (smuggled in pilgrims' hollowed-out staves) to placate the tyrant Justinian, was reserved for the mighty. So was a certain purple dye, unflattering to the Northern European complexion luckily, obtained form shellfish, *Buccinum murex* — not in themselves, you might think, the stuff of wars. Edward VII of England, and far worse his son, George V, were

84

Queen and Goddess — and sacrifice. In 1969, the British Royal Family, one of the last remaining stable monarchies in the world, again felt it necessary to present their eldest son to the restless people of Wales, who were burning down holiday homes, daubing 'Free Wales' on major dams and road signs and muttering about devolution. Again, the dress of absolute Authority was employed. The Queen wore a gold coat which bore virtually no relationship to current fashion, while the Prince, albeit in the robes of his uncle (in democratic times titular rulers should not be seen to be profligate in their expenditure) wore under them full naval dress, having thoroughly earned his stripes. He got a better crown, too, more masterful and authoritative; his wretched uncle had been forced to wear a bandeau more suited for a girl's dancing class. Prince Philip, handsome and dashing as ever, opted for martial glory as princes should, but this time terrestrial not aquatic, since Britannia no longer ruled the waves.

perfectly obsessed with the correctitudes of dress. Since Society was dead set on nipping through the back entrance of erotic style their majesties had to content themselves with roars at their sons and their courtiers for wearing one pip out of order. It should be noted in this precise context that the handsome and enormously ambitious Admiral Beatty regularly wore a décolleté uniform and had his hats blocked to a rakish angle, all very competitive and sexy, and all under

the very nose of his monarch. Perhaps too many medals, or too sure an inheritance, dim the view.

In considering the terror expressed by Authority for desirable dress one must always go back to the roots of the matter. These are imbedded in a fertile compost. In ancient Mediterranean and Nordic cultures, kings had to be killed in order to ensure the harvest and thereby survival. Temporary Kings, as they were called, had to be sacrificed to the common weal, sacrificed unwillingly or willingly. The price of princedom is always to provide success and implicit in success has been a safer and more enjoyable continuation of the race. The 'king', if he is the true leader of his people and not just an imposed or hereditary figurehead, must look to his dress and must look to the dress of those about him for competition in the rôle.

The artist, Felix Topolski, holds a very neat theory about the dress of Authority in its highest form, that is in princedom. First there comes the conqueror, ergonomically dressed in practical armour or simple camouflage jacket, or a uniform with not enough trinkets to get picked out by the enemy as a prime target (Nelson's fatal mistake at Trafalgar; how that gold of martial princedom must have glistened in the sharp-shooter's eye). Shining glamour is necessary to enthuse the troops but fatal for survival, for the King Must Die and be dressed for sacrifice. No wonder earlier kings had permitted three other persons to be dressed on the battlefield identically to themselves, while stomping on other forms of equality in outfit. They wanted to survive and were quite prepared to use dress as a weapon.

Next, according to Topolski, moves in the consolidator who is still in basically working gear, enhanced with the odd bauble. The final decadence, the moment at which it becomes clear to the unthinking mob that the fertility god is dead, is presaged in dress by a figure with medals back and front. Idi Amin? Emperor Bokassa?

To the authority of princes and magnates, it is mass and volume which counts. Victorian aldermen, pompous mayors, cardinals and merchant princes always make quite sure that they are the 'largest' person in the room, for it is this which denotes their power. 'Power is the greatest aphrodisiac' according to Henry Kissinger, but to an increasingly liberated race of women no substitute for a well-cut, manly young chap, which is why menswear is once again going to be exciting and deliberately erotic.

Temporary King. The tyrant Bokassa of the Central African Empire (formerly Republic), whose brutal regime reduced his people to a state of terror and a once comparatively prosperous country to ruin. To emphasise his Authority and therefore 'fertility power', he has adopted a bizarre example of western military dress, though the tastefully disposed gold stars on the sleeves of his jacket would hardly pass muster at Sandhurst or West Point.

The dress of feminine Authority. No-one did it better than Queen Elizabeth I of England, a walking statement of wealth and immortality, but spouses were not far behind. This lady (left) is Louise of Lorraine, the wife of Henry III of France, in 1590. Her dress, though fairly awe-inspiring, is far more pretty than Elizabeth would have worn, for France was greatly influenced by the dulcet Italian styles. The slashing and beading of the over-dress is very sexy, with lots of holes. Her lace is finer and more elaborate than Elizabeth's, coming probably from the Huguenots about to be persecuted by her husband. Elizabeth's lace improved once England gave them shelter.

Man's dress adapted very strictly for a woman has always had a great attraction. In this picture (above) of the Duke and Duchess of Connaught (he was Queen Victoria's son) the Duchess in fact cuts a rather more authoritative figure, dressed as the Colonel-in-Chief of a German regiment, than does her husband, who looks a mite unconvincing in his slung dolman jacket. His boots are suggestive, though, with those long, narrow toes and natty, spurred heels; they must have had to be sewn into place. Her feet look more prosaic.

Sumptuary laws are directly connected to the reservation of the power implicit in dress, and thereby its sexual connotations, to Authority temporal or spiritual. Although there had been constrictions on over-extravagant display, particularly by women in Greece and Rome, by the Middle Ages the whole raison d'être had shifted from the need to appear, at least in public, as democratic. By the Middle Ages the social and status implications of the laws were founded on the precise concept of rulership. By 1776 all but the Poles had given up direct legislation, to the delight of Adam Smith who regarded such interference with a man's due right to self-expression as impertinent.

The conclusion one should draw from the date, though, is that by the eighteenth century most monarchies were established by linear descent, or vaguely so, as opposed to being up for grabs by anyone who caught the popular fancy more than the incumbent, and who was likely to use dress as a major weapon in his attack and so must be

Glory of three kinds. The exquisite and enchanting Princess Alexandra, in a gold lace, off-the-shoulder dress by Belville Sassoon and around £1m of jewellery, greets Louise de la Falaise, aide to Yves St Laurent, at the British Embassy in Paris in 1977. The princess sports the perfect dress to combine fashion with power, for with her sister-in-law, the Duchess of Kent, her style is both iconic and topical. The famed Lulu glitters in the ultimate haute couture interpretation of despotism. Note the red nail on her hand, the delicate colourless shine on the Royal extremity. Smack in the middle, conceding at least to a velvet dinner jacket and somewhat butterfly bow-tie, is the British Ambassador at the time, Sir Nicholas Henderson, symbol of power and Authority.

firmly sat on. One could wade through sheaves of particular anti-dress laws between 1250 and the late eighteenth century, but in fact no stronger statement to uphold the terror of Authority for competitive, i.e. sexually threatening, dress needs to be recalled than the determination exhibited by both sides when the ultimate penalty of public execution was to be enacted.

It was the determination of Authority that felons should be executed having first been denuded, while it was the determination of the powerful who had miscalculated the last shot to be executed in finest fig. One of the most poignant illustrations of this clash must be that by Jacques Callot in his illustrations *Miseries of War*, published in 1633. Called simply 'The Wheel', this terrifying drawing tells you everything about the ultimate danger of the smart gambler. Death on 'the wheel' was a particularly nasty form of public execution, because it was slow. the victim was spread-eagled on a thing like a giant cart-wheel – apparently it was sometimes rotated so that the blows were even less accurate – and then the executioner proceeded to break 'the long bones', i.e. the legs and arms, systematically by thwacking them with an iron pole. It is from this particular form of torture to death that the phrase coup de grâce was coined, since the 'blow of grace', the ultimate stroke to bring merciful death to the pulped body, was very much at the discretion of the paid executioner.

What makes Callot's picture so heart-stopping is that the whole hideous occasion – after all in the early seventeenth century – is shown to be what it was, an exhibition by Authority of public humiliation of the loser, a lesson of agony fit to stop any other

If power resides in dress – and Queen Victoria among others thought that it did – then a man stripped naked is reduced to the commonest felon, his identity and status destroyed. Hence the stripping of criminals for execution, for the hero is seen as merely mortal after all. In Callot's gruesome picture, 'The Wheel', drawn during the religious wars in Lorraine in 1633, the victim, obviously a person of importance, has been so stripped.

89

contender for power in his tracks – and an amazing fashion plate. For all around the elaborate scaffold are ranks of smart, fashionably dressed men, strutting in the high baroque boots and broad-brimmed plumed hats, with sashes and swords and flowing short coats. It is as exciting a spectacle as a matineé with James Bond. And there, because the victim must also have been grand, piled on the corner of the stage set of death, are *his* clothes, his broad-brimmed hat, his sword and coat and sash: naked, all men are stripped to the same level.

Kept too busy with dress, though, plotters can equally be defused. The classic example must be that set by Louis XIV of France, who had everybody so worried about what shape of coat to appear in that they forgot to get together to take over the throne. In 1981 Authority, in the guise of the three-piece-suited this time, managed to get a theory printed in a big-circulation British paper stating that 'love' (it was a family newspaper so they did not use the word 'sex') was too tiring for young executives with their way to make – or a chairmanship to grab. By implication they should now spend so much time dressing in the garb of their portly elders as should render them très dull to the prettier females around.

If Authority in the guise of rulers and legislators and reformers has taken a lot of stick in its attempt to dampen the ardour excited by clothes, it is as nothing compared to the frequently idiotic situation in which the Church has placed herself in pursuit of the same aims. Since Original Sin and, as I have suggested, the initial excuse for erotic dress (concealment) was the invention of Christendom, it follows that it is the Christian Church which was the first to show the whites of its eyes at this naughty new device, fashion. No sooner had a primitive kind of couture evolved than the Church pounced. As hot on the sexual scent as any questing dog, prelates who handily had control over the media of the time got its hacks to work on illustrations of the dangers of style. Your new frock had a pretty train? Turn around, the Devil is sitting on it, you fifteenth-century *Vogue* reader you. That is the price you pay for aping your betters. You might find yourself, after a lot of tiresome fittings, shown up in the village Bible as nothing less than the Devil incarnate, though your designer could have legitimate cause for complaint that you had added wings, horns, and chain-mail digital socks to his original ensemble. Also that your toe-nails were a trifle long.

Down the centuries they tracked. Breasts were definitely out for Abbé Boileau in the late seventeenth century. He composed a treatise with the catchy title, 'A Just and Seasonable Reprehension of Naked Breasts and Shoulders' (one wonders whether any of the good fathers setting up the type wore specs to get steamy at the text, or was there a

90

The Devil attends those who seek to ape their betters by fashionable dress. St Jerome, himself no slouch when it comes to smart hats, admonishes the fiend to leave the lady alone. Why? Because he might be seduced by her charms as emphasised by her pinched waist, long train and stylish headgear?

sharp fight for the wood-cuts?). Abbé Boileau, who may have been peeking at his parishioners – how else would he know? – warned that the sight of a beautiful bosom is as dangerous as that of a basilisk (and that evil-eyed serpent is indeed a sex-symbol to be reckoned with).

If the State was nervous about dress, the Christian Church was positively panicked by its implications for here they confronted not just a threat to their power but a threat to their pastoral/moral duties too. Having successfully fig-leaved Adam and Eve into genital obscurity and so unwittingly started off the whole hunt for What's Underneath, they moved quickly to prevent any suggestion that Jesus Christ, although made man, might have had the usual manly physical equipment. As I have said, to remove the victim's clothing is the ultimate degradation which Authority can inflict prior to torture and an agonising death (at both of which the Christian Church has shown itself remarkably adept) and Jesus, rejected by his own people, who were squeamish about the body, and committed to rough Roman justice, was very likely crucified naked as was the practice with common criminals. After all, we know that the soldiers divided the clothing of the victims as part of their perks for an unpleasant task. But none of the gospels mentions underwear, and so one must assume that as was the custom for the time and place, Our Lord wore nothing under his seamless caftan.

Under the general panic of religion, there is no area of the human body and no garment which has not been outcast at some time or other for the quite simple reasons that they impinged on the dangerous grounds of sensuality. Of course there was another side to the Church's demolition of high style, but that fits really under its

This picture of two smart French ladies, Gabrielle d'Estrées and the Duchesse de Villars, has been labelled by posterity with all sorts of lesbian overtones which are quite inaccurate: just as in the late nineteenth century, when make-up was still taboo except for whores, girls were pinching their cheeks and biting their lips to produce an enticing 'natural' colour, so 300 years earlier the girls were applying the same technique to parts liable to be admired by gentlemen shortly. Will the nuns, a far cry from the French court circle, approve the picture for culture's sake and to show the modern Church's broad-mindedness, or will they react with feelings of distaste which would reflect the Church's traditional response to all things blatantly sexual?

rôle as lords temporal, dedicated, like any prince, to the maintenance of their status. As lords spiritual, the Church credited the failure of the French at Crécy not to English long-bowmen but to the 'arrogant immodesty of dress seen everywhere about the kingdom'. Moving in a trice, the Church hauled Murillo the painter before the Inquisition for showing the Virgin Mary as having toes, and deplored the invention of buttons – particularly funny when one considers that lots of tempting covered buttons are now the prerogative of the habit of the Roman Catholic Church. As for covering the hair, well, like toes, at many seasons the Church has decreed that the privilege of that viewing so intimate a part presupposes carnal knowledge of the owner of said part.

The Church was never too keen on waists, hips, bosoms: you anatomise it, they will have anathematised it some time or other. The Church was particularly anti-shoe, which has been of course the most overtly phallic exhibit in menswear. Having castigated the wearers of those long-toed numbers in the fourteenth century, they were still firing vicars in 1970 for wearing 'winkle-pickers', very narrow, pointed shoes with obvious alternative phallic implications. Indeed the proper motto for religion à propos dress ought to be honi soit qui mal y pense — shame be to him who evil thinks – because the prelates seem to have seen it all about them.

It is tempting to assume that the Church's interference was confined to either long ago or far away. Not at all. In the early 1920s, in Holland of all places, the women were shocked by clean-shaven priests – the beard has always been a sign of Authority – and the

92

priests were shocked by short hair, short skirts and uncovered arms and legs. Eline Canter Cremers-van der Does, in her excellent book, *The Agony of Fashion,* records that one young priest was moved even unto an emulation of the rôle of Poiret. Dutch bishops, writing in 1926, expected that the faithful should be covered from head to toe and also join a Society of Honour and Virtue, membership of which included exposure to a publication entitled *Fashion Chats.* This was pretty startling stuff, not quite your women's magazine cosy approach.

Written by an anonymous priest, *Fashion Chats* describes in detail the death in 1921 of a young girl, victim of an immoral fashion. She had died, it seems, of a chill on the kidneys brought about by short skirts, but since skirts were not then so very short one should take this as merely another repressive attempt. It may be, though, that the author was a frustrated designer, for he goes on to specific recommendations for an outfit, modelled on his mother's, which turns out to be a stately gown of black velvet covered in jet beads. Note the insistence on pomp and glitter and at the same time the suggestion of a dress so heavy that dancing the Charleston (i.e. female flight from the predator) would have been chicly impossible. Woman would again have been correctly bonded to man, à la mode and so happy with her lot.

By 1928 a Dutch magazine called *The Catholic Woman* was running frisky fashion sketches with everyone in short skirts and Eton crops and funniest touch of all, the once-deplored styles are given the official imprimatur by the artist's inclusion, centre stage, of the obligatory child, thus saying in so many words that you can be smart and yet a proper Catholic propagator. Within ten years of the anonymous priest's admonitions about black velvet and lots of beads women were wearing just that; but not courtesy of him, courtesy of the great vamps of the movie screen.

This seems a shame. If the Pope can be merchandised or pre-packed for his travels by a top managing agent to the point of giving rise to cartoons about whether we could expect Pope-endorsed T-shirts (what would they have on the front? Correspondence with King Henry VIII?) why should not other clergymen be encouraged to provide strict sartorial guidelines? It was always rumoured that several of the collections shown by the Italian haute couture group were the work of priests moonlighting from the Vatican. For Churches which have lost their followings and their status it could be a most handy source of extra income. Masses of people still yearn for definitive direction on dress, even if rather lax about accepting definitive directions on things spiritual and on how much to put in the plate on Sundays. Fashion writers, swinging with the tide, have

The Roman Catholic Church made a grave mistake in trying to move closer to the people in its dress. It invited famed Paris designers such as Pierre Cardin to provide alternative clothing, but when the faithful find out that nuns' feet hurt, too, once they get into fashion shoes, where is the mystery? Where the divine power? This mish-mash of ancient and modern simply doesn't work.

abandoned their flocks to 'do your own thing with your wardrobe' just as many priests have abandoned their flocks to do their own thing with their God. Some strong words from the pulpit again on the iniquities of not wearing gloves might be just the thing.

Sadly, though, the established Church, at any rate in most of Europe and America, has made a cardinal error in its own dress. It has opted for the dress of the people, imagining that in this way it will bring them closer together. They should have stuck with the panoply of power. I greatly doubt whether worshippers really want to see nuns de-frocked; the designer, Hardy Amies, once told me that the most erotic sight of dress he had ever seen was properly garbed nuns playing tennis, wimples and all. Do you suppose their gym shoes were black?

Then, who wants to see priests wandering around rubbing their hands emolliently and looking like you and me in our gardening clothes? Combatant and doughty as they are, the established Churches ought to take a close look at the sartorial appeal of all these sinister and some say highly dangerous religious cults which are springing up all around us in the 1980s. They should take note that the dress of the leaders is the panoply of power, of mass, of Authority. They should do as any wise monarch should now do, and remove themselves utterly from the everyday fashion. Kings should revert to icon figures, spiritual leaders to mysterious and closely privileged robing.

The area of Authority which I have left until last concerns the guardians of our health. I have left it till last because quite frankly it

94

The following labels appear within the cartoon: "I can't sit down", "18 83", "INSTRUMENT OF TORTURE", "THE WIGGLE-WAGGLE", "TIGHT TROUSERS & STAYS", "THE HIGH COLLAR", "THE MIRACULOUS WAIST"

Society has dodged around the demands of Authority and economic necessity in its determination to survive by being attractive to the opposite sex. To do so it has incurred serious risks, not least to health, and this cartoon of 1883 makes fun of this aspect of the prevailing fashions. Compare the man's tight, high collar and stiff, extended neck to the ringed African beauty shown on page 55.

has never had the slightest effect on clothing in the mass sense. Despite producing irrefutable proof that followers of fashion would catch pneumonia, displace their inner organs, risk miscarriage, consumption, heart attacks, bunions and the nine dread diseases listed by a speaker at the yearly general meeting of Roman Catholic physicians in 1925, the medical profession and the reformers hell-bent on hygiene have been dismally unsuccessful in alerting Society to obey their very sensible suggestions, right down the ages.

In the case of the medical profession, this can be explained quite candidly. They have a living to make, and nagging at customers about things that they do not wish to hear or believe is quite a short cut to insolvency. The National Health Service, which might be expected to be dispassionate about its advice, has, so far as I am aware, made no general comments on dangerous clothing still worn in order to attract the opposite sex.

As for the reformers, they forgot in their woolly-mindedness the basic principle of dress, which is vanity and eroticism. Dr Gustav Jaeger captured only a groupie following except by mistake in countries where woollen underwear was a necessity for survival. On the practical level, reform clothes tended to be the work of artists and while admirable in concept never caught on with the mass manu-facturers, who found them impossibly impractical to make. But above all they were not what the public wanted. They had intel-lectual, not sexual appeal. Clever designers combine both.

Confronted by the implacable determination of Church and State to rule in dress as in everything else and to stamp out displays of moral, i.e. sexual, superiority, or at any rate to reserve it exclusively to those in power, Society in general did what Society always does if it is to survive. It learned to dissemble. No sooner had the good priests or failing kings detected a threat in fashion and outlawed such a style than ingenious mankind devised a new signalling system for the age-old message. Obviously, the more repressive the regime, the more subtle had to be the sartorial red herrings. Quite extraordinary feats of imagination were employed to deflect attention to areas of the body which seemed to those in power ineluctably respectable. By the time the monitors had caught on to the surrogate sexual implications of the style, fashion, the silent cry of the individual and an eternal tease to the gallumphing mighty, had decided that that particular vogue was old hat.

It was the short haul to hypocrisy. Society invented a vocabulary of fashion, if you like, which is as arcane as semaphore or that amazing chit-chat of Citizens Band radio communication. All three are designed to get messages across to interested and sympathetic parties while at the same time defeating the attempts of Authority to decode until it is too late and the frequency has been changed.

The most simple way for Society to get away with wearing practically anything, or practically nothing, was to pretend that their fashions were inspired by some great bygone age. Thus when confronted with accusations of indecency they could pretend an innocent hauteur towards anyone who complained. Since not even the mighty, let alone the slaves of convention, were keen to be sneered at by the trendsetters as boorish and illiterate provincials, the most extraordinary displays of flesh have been permitted under the justification that they were 'classically inspired'.

To promote this handy ruse a great increase in travel or a great increase in literature describing other apparently admirable lifestyles needed to be available to the fashion-conscious public; either that or some perceptive and informative fashion editors, but these were only available after World War II; up till then, the huddle masses at any rate had to be content with gawping, copying and minding their sartorial Ps and Qs.

A perfectly splendid example of Society getting away with scandalously sensual dress was provided by the period after the French Revolution (1789). Fashion is always at its most provocative during or after times of war, for the excellent reason that, from the woman's point of view, there is more than a good chance of a lot of eligible males turning up their toes at any minute (one night the Duchess of Richmond's Ball, the next day carnage at Waterloo) so speed was of the essence in the sexual come-on message. Men at war

stance, which to an extent is brought about by confidence in dress and a sure sense of identity, but is inherent in certain males, is very attractive to many women. It is the similarity of pose as much as the polar extremes of outfit which make this picture so interesting as a study of the appeal of menswear. The British policeman on the left is exceptionally handsome and well built, the sort of fellow to protect the nesting female. On the right, the Rastafarian has adopted Western dress but with a colour and individual panache which still suggests that, though far from Ethiopia, if you were his mate your return from the supermarket would be trouble-free.

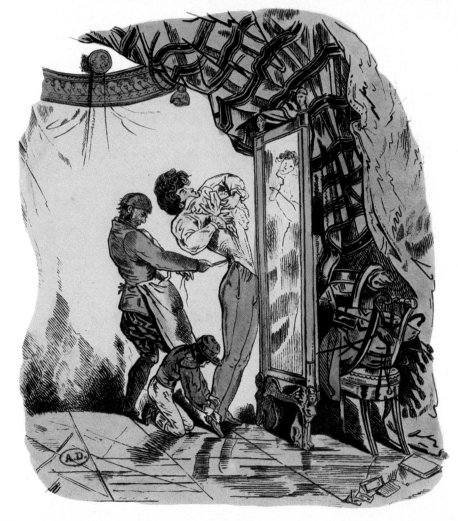

If a small waist is a sign originally of fecundity and later of submission to man's taste in women, what does the small waist signify in men? Initially, tight binding served a useful purpose, supporting the torso on exhausting military campaigns, and so became associated with martial glamour and a sense of power. In the days of short life-expectancy, that martial glamour was likely to be associated with youth, not with pot-bellied generals waging war from the safety of a few hundred miles. The small waist on a man denotes the desire for a youthful and virile appearance, and men have been at almost as much pain to achieve it by their own desire as have the 'second sex' by the requirements of the 'first sex'. This is a French cartoon of about 1830.

Tissot's magnificent portrait of Frederick Gustavus Burnaby, painted in 1870, says it all about the clothes of a certain type of very grand, very blasé British cavalry officer, although with his books and his chintzes, his waxed moustache and his beautiful hands, he is a far cry from the stylish louts from other regiments whose pants were too tight to let them dance. In the background are the accoutrements of battle which had been obsolete since the invention of gunpowder as any form of protection, but which retained a magic allure that gave both bravery to the wearer and a big thrill to the quavering ladies he was off to protect.

With his tough, working-class posture, lyrics which were hardly taxing or liable to cause alarm to any generation, his cheerful, carolling voice and his bouncy, optimistic presence, but above all with his clothes, Adam Ant (left) became the British rock idol of the 1980s. Had he stood up and yodelled the telephone directory none of his myriad fans would have minded, because lodged at the back of their minds as he blasted their way through breakfast or Sony Walkmanned their way to school, they had the visual image of their hero, dressed in just the sort of junk they felt like wearing – uniforms, bits of pirate gear, highwayman stuff – but always gallant, always the hero. Sight travels faster than sound. Adam Ant's clothes cost hundreds of pounds and a lot of time to work out, but the same sexy appeal was available from the jumble sales if you knew what you were looking for.

The Establishment way with colourful dress (above). This alderman, like other pillars of English society, is no less ornately dressed than the rock star; however, the appeal of his clothes is not only that they exude power but that they represent a soothing continuity in which you have no choice, whereas for the pop star and his followers it depends on personal initiative.

The conqueror can afford simplicity, while surrounding himself with an entourage so splendid that they set off his own unique position. Thus Napoleon enters Berlin, as painted by Meynier, in a plain green field coat, unbraided hat and busy making democratic gestures (left). His determination to consolidate his reign is however implicit in the power dress of those accompanying him. Meynier has even painted the horse's ears impossibly small so that they look like the corners of a victor's laurel wreath (though this might be unintentional in view of anatomical deficiencies in the rest of the beast, whose hind legs look more like those of Napoleon than a charger).

LE PETIT JOURNAL ILLUSTRÉ

PARAISSANT LE DIMANCHE
40° Année - N° 1987
On s'abonne dans tous les bureaux de poste
Les Manuscrits ne sont pas rendus

ABONNEMENTS
Trois mois Six mois Un an
FRANCE & COLONIES
6 fr.   12 fr.   24 fr.
ÉTRANGER (tarif ordinaire)
8 fr.   16 fr.   32 fr.
ANGLETERRE ET SUISSE
10 fr.   20 fr.   40 fr.

POUR UNE JUPE TROP COURTE...

A most ambiguous cartoon, given the Church's normally repressive attitude to fashion, for here the priest is seen protecting a lady whose dress by its shortness and chic has offended the reactionary elements of French peasant society. Since it is dated 1929 and skirts had previously been a great deal shorter, it is a joke both at the expense of the Church, anxious to support the wealthy (fur collar and cuffs), and at the expense of boring lower-class persons, around whose attitudes Society has dodged in the quest for attractive dress as efficiently as it has around those of Authority.

FULL DRESS

Pub.d 24 Nov.r 1799 by S.t W. Fores, N.o 50, Piccadilly.

Folies of Caricatures bound for the Evening

PARISIAN LADIES in their WINTER DRESS for 1800

Attempts by the Church to impose 'decency' in dress have continued virtually up to the present day, with hirers-out of mantillas and dusty cardigans to be found outside the great religious tourist spots, eager to inform the lobster-coloured visitors that they cannot go inside showing so much bare flesh. This caricature, printed in 1798, pokes fun at the Durham Inquest, in fact a serious enquiry into ecclesiastical matters which was rash enough to venture into fields of fashion by suggesting what was appropriate wear. The cartoon shows on the right the German reaction to this hilarious peep-show, as the figure looking into the mirror, and wearing hideous dress and padded legs, remarks, 'Oh, vat fright! I vonder vat figure dey vill make of Bacchus, dis is vat dey call a *Divine* dress, eh?'

The real risks of high fashion: Society is always prepared to take them, it seems, in the hop, skip and dance of sexual survival. These dresses if you can believe it are *winter* dresses for Paris in 1800 (the heyday of the classical influence in post-Revolution France) and since one of the women is wearing a bonnet, one must assume that such wildly inappropriate garb for the freezing slush of northern Europe was not intended for the ballroom. Exaggerated though this German caricature may be, it does illustrate the lengths to which Society is prepared to go to be alluring. It also illustrates a neat contradiction, for though the ladies are dressed with Grecian abandon, they are also wearing ankle decorations reminiscent of the stepping-chains of the totally veiled women of the Middle East.

Not since the Regency period had women worn such blatantly transparent clothes outside the bedroom as they began to in the mid-1970s. A whole era of innocent tease dresses – now you see it, now you don't – was ushered in along with the rafts of cheap Indian cotton dresses, made in the thinnest muslin, which struck Europe and North America at that time. Their price and their prettiness were irresistible, as was the delightful softness of their texture on the skin in hot weather. Though usually lined by the respectable Indian makers and printed in patterns, this only added to the excitement because men could hope that a blank bit might work out over a nipple. What was more, all of a sudden girls had legs all the way up. The underwear industry was thrown into confusion as stout matrons desired to be both fashionable and respectable, and at public gatherings elderly men could be seen purpling as young gels insouciantly revealed that there was little underneath their drifting dresses, while at the same time the lady-wife was revealing defences suitable for the Somme when talking by the window. These dresses are by Zandra Rhodes, in pure silk chiffon, and were in her spring 1980 collection.

Transparency may be all very well for the sophisticated, but peasant societies had to create a more devious method of teasing attention to the legs. Since Authority in Spain was reluctant even to admit that women had legs, it was from Spain and, as a result of its conquering influence, from South America that the Frills came. The sexual pointer is as obvious as a rosette on a shoe, the frills (under or over a skirt which is always narrow over the loins) signifying the pubic hair and the labia. The French, of course, commercialised the idea in the can-can, and by the 1970s Society had turned the whole thing into a joke, and a very pretty one, too (above).

Venus arising from the waves (above), and offering as her fertility symbol a peeled-down banana with lots more to come. Bathing suits were not around when Botticelli painted his version of the Goddess of Love in 1478 (right), so he made do with a few wisps of hair about as concealing as this modern swimwear design, and he gave her as accessories the fruits of the sea, not of a tropical tree. The message is the same, though, and on the plus side (due no doubt to superior feeding over the last 500 years), current bathing beauties do not have knock knees.

have the inbuilt advantage of uniform, the sexual connotations of which have been discussed elsewhere.

But how to make the best of those, possibly last, moments? Consider the times. Faced with a crucial need to be even more erotically stimulating, fashion, or at any rate the surviving Society which creates it, takes a quick look round and then a very big jump away from what has gone before. The greater the need, the more the over-reaction. In late eighteenth-century France, the world of itsy-bitsy, lace-ruffled, multi-skirted, laced, tied, buttoned and bowed, giggling, ultra-feminine elegance (for both sexes, it must be said), with wigs and muffs and heaven knows what resorts to titillation of the bored and ineffectual, had been guillotined. A new spirit was abroad, but some quick thinking was in order if the smarties were to turn this rather ominous political situation to their own sexual advantage.

Right on hand for anyone with their eyes open, and this is after all what survival is all about, was the Glory of the Ancient World. Not only had knowledge of exotic places become much more widely available as the intrepid travellers of the eighteenth century became more likely to survive their travels and to live to recount them in equally intrepid prose, but the hero, or anti-hero of the hour, depending which side you were on, Napoleon Bonaparte, was fresh

The most decent indecency. Showing a scantily clad woman in a 'classical' role has been a typical trick of Society to dodge conventional or authoritarian ruling. Seated upon a wine cask, with ivy leaves entwined in her hair (who would know that they are not from the vine?), and holding aloft not a bunch of grapes to be crushed into the mouth but a bunch of flowers which if eaten might cause a painful demise, this Bacchante of 1880 epitomises nineteenth-century hypocrisy.

returned from fights on the edges of the classical world. 'Soldiers, from the summit of these pyramids forty centuries look down upon you,' the little Corsican exhorted his troops in 1798 prior to one of them blowing off the nose of the Sphinx by mistake. With such romance wafting down from on high, who should be surprised that model matrons all of a sudden appeared in transparent white gauzes à la Grecque, heroic and classless. This dissembly – any Grecian matron would have been cast out of Athens, chiton and all, for such rudeness – cost not a few lives sacrificed to sexiness in a chill northern climate, but then sensual fashion will always pay the price.

In its determination to remain always one skip ahead of Authority in the Dance of Dress, Society through the ages has shown itself quite remarkably calm to the danger that it may be cavorting to the Dance of Death as well. Fearful prices to be sure might have to be paid in economic terms – the confiscation of estates, the forfeiture of titles, exile, to say nothing of social ostracism and a great degree of family sharp-tonguing (popular among Royalty of Germanic background), excommunication, demotion, redundancy – trifles such as these were and are commonplace to those who flouted their superiors.

But to be fashionable, which is in the context of this book to be also sexually alluring, carried real physical danger, too. At the extreme, too bold a display of competitive status, always implicit in dress, could well lead to the scaffold. At the most bizarre, too keen an application to the demands of erotic stimulation have led to death or nearly to death. The most famous and familiar examples of both can be attributed to the mid-sixteenth century. Since Spain under the church-ridden Philip II was rich and powerful, it set a certain style, which could at kindest be called repressive. Everyone wore black or sombre colours, and women were regarded as the work of the Devil, their breasts especially suspect. Into the bodices of little girls were sewn lead weights to repress growth. Women were padded from head to foot, every female physical characteristic obliterated. In desperation, the more lusty of the King's entourage – after all, they were engaged in the New World, in capturing and conquering, in fighting the Netherlands and in mounting the Armada, all fairly virile pursuits, one way and another – in desperation, as I say, the more spirited lads developed a cult for that portion of the anatomy which stood the most sporting chance of being uncovered: the foot. Ha-ha, said Authority, not even a peep of toe may be displayed. Carriages shall have curtains specially designed to be let down when a woman descends in case anyone should by chance get a peek of her shod foot, let alone her real toes.

With Cupid at the prow and Authority at the helm, it is small wonder that the foot developed into an absolute mania in sex-starved

Spain. The sight of the foot at all, let alone an undressed foot, was the exclusive preserve of the husband, referred to, as were and are all things of sexual style, in French as la dernière faveur. To accomplish this 'faveur', if you were not the husband, was to court death, for either party as it turns out. The Queen of Spain was thrown from her horse and dragged by her stirrup towards certain death as the terrified animal bolted at a great review. The Spanish Establishment watched helpless because to disentangle HRH would have necessitated not just seeing, but touching, the Royal foot. Thus she would have been killed for a fashionable demand, had not two gentlemen had the gallantry to risk the Royal wrath, the Church's opprobrium and social ostracism by spurring to her side and disentangling her. Pragmatic modernists would have suggested that in view of the penalty which awaited their altruistic efforts they should have borrowed a leaf out of classical doctrine and done a Perseus/Medusa job with mirrors, while liberated ladies will wish to know what all those silly vapid maids of honour were doing, just sitting around and gawping. But of course, their effecting the rescue might have entailed showing their feet. Anyway, what happened was that the two gents galloped off into the sunset, or in fact into the nearest monastery, to seek asylum from immediate execution, absolution (with lots of very sexy penances, no doubt) and dreams of that tiny, Royal foot.

It seems that the royal pardon was forthcoming, which is more than can be said for one of their equally frustrated contemporaries. Falling under the charms of a lady visitor, this fellow, who really must have been high on the invisibility kick, staged a most expensive accident (he burned down his house) so that he could save the object of his desires. Unfortunately he was spotted by his page caressing the forbidden foot and, betrayed, was shot by the husband. All this before the days of household insurance, too.

Calculated danger is of course itself very erotic, which is why everybody goes on arguing about whether Victorian women really wanted to wear corsets or not. There is no argument about the effects of wearing corsets. They were disastrous, as painful as any bodily mutilation and in their own special way far more damaging. While the decorative and erotically stimulating effects of body scoring had all the marks of submission or bravery with their associated charms, the corset mutilated the body not only exernally but internally. Of this the wearers, of both sexes, were well aware had they cared to be. They cared not to be, and the chronicle of illnesses endured in the wake of fashion is common reading. Less common is the report in the newspapers in 1980 that the 'revival' of the mini-skirt could give rise to a chill on the kidneys. Did anyone say that in 1965? No. Authority only catches up with fashion flops.

Above left: Society found much mirth in masked balls, for it enabled very precarious and unsuitable costumes to be worn under the guise of anonymity. No wonder that the sign at the back says 'Horns to Sell', the masquerade being the most likely opportunity for cuckolding. The lady on the right could have done with pincushion pads in her drawers, like the lady on the Paris Métro illustrated on page 44.

Above right: The top echelon of Society at sexual play again. The Duke of Connaught disguised with great humour – intentional or unintentional – as the Beast for the fancy dress ball given by the Prince and Princess of Wales in 1874 (it is to be assumed that the Duchess went as Beauty). Since it was in July, the Duke has wisely opted not for the whole furry outfit but for more of a transformation scene involving an Arthurian princely ensemble, one of the rugs from Windsor Castle and a fetching hat no doubt run up by Rowland Ward or the equivalent ace taxidermist of the time.

The other great escape route for Society doomed by its superiors to toe the line in dress has been to hold costume balls. These are not without their own terrors, since on appearing in a mask at a party in Venice in 1924 the renowned beauty, Lady Diana Cooper, was summarily expelled because she was wearing a mask, and recent sumptuary laws enacted by the authorities there had outlawed such dangers, though I do not know why. Another danger was to be sent up mercilessly, as by the famous Edwardian diarist, Eton master and Master of Magdalene, Arthur Benson, who was keen to compare overdressed pomposities as looking like 'a grocer at a fancy-dress ball'. Society however persisted, particularly during times of restraint by authoritative opinion which had little physical backing, such as the period from the nineteenth century onwards in Western Europe.

Since it is always peasant dress which is the most erotic, peasants being hard-working people with little time for the niceties of foreplay and a strong sense of wanting to know what they are going to be getting, a popular outfit for costume ball-goers – and indeed for Royal families who were stifled with contemporary dress – was a highly modified version of what toilers in the field and rompers in the barn might have been wearing. Since nobody in the ball-going Royal sets was all that keen on being identified as a peasant, the outfit was interpreted as 'National Dress'. Green or scarlet baize gave way to softest lace for the stomacher and blouse, coarse leather to velvet for the deliciously low-cut, laced overbodice. The gentlemen on the whole were less keen to adopt rustic clothing, National Dress or no,

One hundred years after the French Revolution had seemed to render such japes against the working class outmoded, the fancy dress ball at Devonshire House produced a spate of *faux paysannes*. The enchanting ladies Churchill turned up as Watteau shepherdesses, and were about as removed from the stout guardians of the flock in real life as was Marie Antoinette playing games at Le Petit Trianon. But the allure is irresistible: the charming, pretty, virgin country girl, her laced corselet all set for the undoing.

and tended to clomp about in the – equally stimulating – dress not of fertility but of power: bits and pieces of armour and that sort of thing. When not opting for peasant garb, the ladies were very keen on appearing as non-persons – Night, Dawn, Justice – which gave them a pretty free rein to show off the bits of themselves they thought most of, or as goddesses, which amounted to much the same thing.

Several psychologists and commentators, including Simone de Beauvoir, have alleged that women, either earlier or in middle age, are suddenly seized by a desire to expose themselves to the public. This is not the explanation provided by Bernard Rudofsky, the psychologist, for the startling ensemble selected by the future Duchess of Kingston for a diplomatic party in 1749. She came, as she thought, dressed as Iphigenia, ready for sacrifice, and was wearing so little that Horace Walpole thought she must be trying to look like Andromeda, while another spiteful diarist pointed out that the perpetrator of the sacrifice would have no difficulty in inspecting the entrails of the offering.

For a handsome young woman, all set to become a duchess and stuck in the convention of dress demanded by a Maid of Honour, it would seem that the insatiable desire to freak into costume had got the better of her. Rudofsky however maintains that hers was an early plea for women's liberation against clothes and men. Since she succeeded in discarding the former and hooking the latter, whatever her motives her gown must be counted an erotic success.

After World War I there came another vogue for dressing-up parties. Two features are noticeable. The number of transvestite

101

In theory, see-through fabrics were a tease but in this instance the blatancy defeats the object of sensual dressing which is to leave the attracted party guessing. It is the innocent, or apparently innocent, exposure which baits the trap. Blatancy is for the voyeur, who would quite probably be inadequate physically or financially to do anything about it anyway.

costumes selected by both sexes represented a residue of homo-sexuality from the war, and the first chance to express true feelings by pretending that it was a game. The second was circus parties. One does not have to look hard to find the erotic connotations of guests performing under the whip of a female ringmaster. Again, it was Society's comment on things to come.

Nowadays, everybody dresses up. Still Authority is terrified, seeing punks, rockers, flower children as threats to their rule.

A handsome young man of my acquaintance makes it a point to lunch with an old (male) friend in the City of London on an annual basis of the last week in May. The reason is simple: the girls will be out in their summer dresses. Summer dresses are, oh, so sweet: transparent cheesecloths and sheer batistes, Indian summer for any mind, natty little crisp washing frocks, split thigh-high for coolness, of course.

There are two sorts of tease, or are there really three? There is innocence, a display of body which Society allows. Puritan house-holds frown on a dart from bedroom to bathroom in bra and panties without benefit of dressing wrap, yet even the Spanish beach police will now let you wear very much or less the same in full view of a thousand sun-scorched strangers.

These are the two sides of revelation in an acceptable sense. In the case of the fine fabric frock, the tease is in the unconscious. They thought in their innocence that the print would hide their nipples so that they need not wear a bra, the satiny cotton caressed their skin, absorbed sweat effortlessly. That it was so soft that it wrapped itself around their thighs and between their legs was lost to their fashion-able view, but not to that of the voyeur.

The dress for active sport presents another simply splendid occasion for physical display which no-one can object to. In outlaw-ing colour the Wimbledon authorities once again give us a delicious example of sexy Society footing it in advance of a lot of choleric-complexioned retired service persons. Of course, we'll wear white, so pure and proper, not likely to frighten elderly members, all very genteel. The hilarious fact of the matter is that while the dresses may be white, with all its tremendously exciting symbolism of virginity and untouched pleasures for the conqueror, the clothes themselves are of such brevity, masculinity, feminity or sheer power implication that there have to be special sittings of magistrates' courts during the All-England Championships to deal with the rash of usually respect-able persons arrested for trying out some vicarious bum-rubbing on whoever is next to them in the crowded stands.

Then there are bathing suits. Innocence is poised on the diving board in a child-like, navy-blue, school-regulation costume. Lolita-

A fascinating contradiction in terms between the image expected of a public figure on duty and how she sees herself privately. In the mid-1970s the distinguished British tennis player, Virginia Wade, was wearing frilly drawers, a tidy dress and a neat bow in her chignon to appear at Wimbledon while displaying in her game, as this picture shows, the aggressive power — and the legs — more usually associated with a man. Since revelations about the private life of several circuit stars, Miss Wade has turned to boyish separates on court and has had her hair shorn into a tumble of curls Byronic.

103

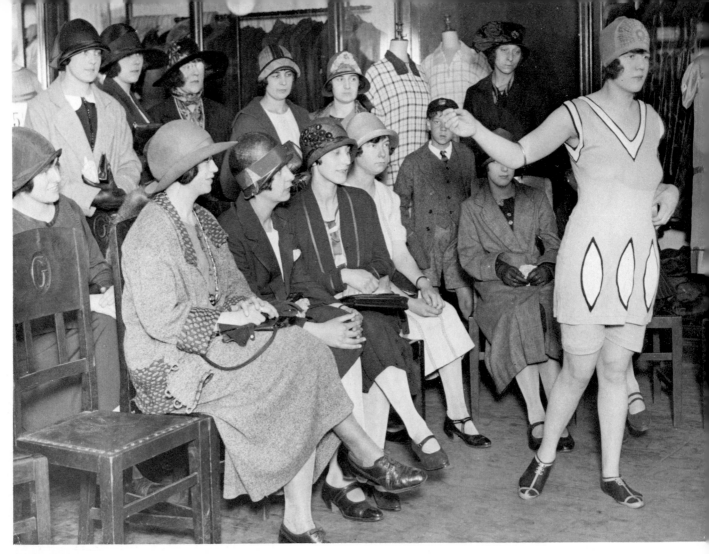

Swimwear and sportswear have always provided an opportunity for display of the body which would otherwise be considered unacceptable in public. In 1925 the department store, Gamages, close to the centre of London and thus a good location for the newly emancipated business girls of the period, started to hold lunch-hour fashion parades. This sensible ensemble would have been practical for the freezing waters most swimmers encountered before the era of the package tour to the Costa Brava. But sexy?

sized breasts, tiniest whisk of blond pubic hair, and all the school governors are mopping their brows and heading for the nearest showing of the movie, *Pretty Baby*. Sophistication pads the Astroturf around the heated pool, or pretends to gambol with a beach ball in a way which will not upset her coiffeur while leaving nothing of her body to the imagination. Or she is deliberately aggressive and muscular in her play – a wrestling companion worth the fight, perhaps?

The everlasting clashes between Authority and Society have produced some memorable examples of fashion double-talk. The two supreme ones must be, for men, the wearing of the codpiece, and for women, the wearing of mini-skirts. Both are instances of Society thumbing its nose at Authority by turning an apparently shocking item of clothing into a convenient bit of decoration, while moving the erogenous interest elsewhere.

In the fourteenth century the development of stockings, or at any rate very close-fitting leg-apparel, for men coincided with a fashion for very short tunics. This left some very interesting technical matters to be resolved — for example, just what was to be attached to what,

and how — and also provided some jazzy opportunities for genital display, hitherto impossible with baggy drawers under capacious robes, or just baggy drawers. It also provided some jazzy opportunities for things to split, come off too easily, fall down, and generally leave the gentleman in indecent disarray. Possibly none the worse for it, either.

The Christian Church, which had been having a great run-in over shoes with toes so long that they could be used to poke up ladies' skirts under the dinner-table (how unromantic we are, kicking them off at the first opportunity) and were generally far, far too sexy, now turned its attention to the real, not the putative phallus. The unacceptable bits of the old Adam must be properly covered, Authority decreed. Persons must not skip about inciting licentious thoughts. A decent extra covering must be produced which would mask the offending part.

'Anything to oblige' was the reply and, after a short space of neat jock-straps, the codpiece became an accepted form of dress and thus liable to elaboration. In fact, it was elaborated into something as pretentious as the natural attributes of any pagan fertility symbol.

By the era of the package tour to St Tropez this sight was becoming common, since it is the resorts favoured by the young and chic which set the trends for the masses now. Lips pursed in horror — you can almost hear her saying 'Mon Dieu' or 'Well I never' — the older woman has abandoned any attempt at physical allure. Nevertheless, she has not abandoned the dress of her status as a respectable matron: even in the sea she is carrying the sceptres of handbag and shopping bag. By far the best bathing suits are available in America, where no matter what your size or shape, you can buy something pretty and flattering.

105

In the background the phallic lighthouse, symbol of hope and continuing life, also of rugged manpower; in the foreground the modern equivalent of Iphigenia, dedicated to safety on the seas by her father and carrying a suitably sacrificial garland. Despite the mini-skirt, she looks both innocent and well armoured.

What is more, when not serving the practical functions which it had always done in battle, mock or real, but used as a bow to respectability, it was tremendously useful as a purse, in which to tuck small odds and ends before the days of pockets and handbags. Thus what is usually viewed with excitement when its outline is indicated (notably in sport or war), when imposed on to the fashion-conscious public became no more sexual than the sporran of the Scots or of the seventeenth-century French noblemen.

My second example of erotic defusing is much more modern but equally complex, and equally initiated by social change and by prevailing moral winds. I refer to the arrival among respectable Society of the mini-skirt.

Very short skirts have by tradition been the preserve of the theatre or the whore-house; something to be sanctified in the cause of art (always so obliging an excuse) or used for a quite deliberate provocation. In the mid-1960s Authority in the guise of science, with its invention of the Pill, and Authority in the guise of the lifting of so many political and economic sanctions hitherto imposed on women, resulted in the haute couture mini. Tarts had worn it, chorus dancers had worn it, freaky Kings Roaders had worn it to tease but suddenly, here were princesses and Board chairpersons showing their knees (and, much worse, the backs of their knees) to all and sundry.

That they got away with it was because the whole sexual fuse was damped by the introduction of tights. The mini presented the observer with expectations of a glimpse of flesh, that most erotic area between thigh and pudenda, the most delicately skinned and sensitive patch of skin on a woman's body. It suggested that here at last, in a smart drawing-room, he might with all these liberated women around – who were presumably as free to be laid as they were with their opinions on how to run his company, on his virility and on how they expected him to help wash the dishes – that he might glimpse hitherto forbidden delights. Not a bit of it. Once the mini-skirt became accepted high fashion, tights – decent, chaste and convenient – doomed it as an erotic garb. Society had survived by compromise yet again.

But what had unquestionably occurred at this stage was a confrontation of the professional (i.e. the prostitute) and the amateur in seductive dressing. As moral standards tumbled like plates in a china-smashing stall, or to be more generous, as the human spirit was able more freely to express its sexual longings in dress, as Psyche might see Cupid in daylight without death, so the professional catering to exotic tastes found that the demands made on her (or him) were likely to be of a more exotic nature, since the amateurs were having a go at practically everything else, clothed to suit.

106

Thus one finds in the past twenty-five years not only a selection of surprisingly frank literature and advertisements for what would formerly have been deemed reserved dress – eight-inch heeled shoes in size 12 advertised in a quality Sunday newspaper, for example – but a very small degree of shock at homosexual dressing. Women dressed overtly to attract other women, men to attract men; with increasing over-population in the Western world, the concept of non-productive relationships is no longer quite taboo.

Society at large – and in that sense I mean a society which is free – must always remain the arbiter of what is attractive in dress, for it is the attractive that is stimulating. Society at large remains the tribal notice-board, whether it be for straights or for gays (what colour handkerchief, your preferences signalled by the side you hang your keys).

The interesting thing will be to see, now that everyone is free to dress up and so that fun channel has been dammed, just what turn it will take. The only sure thing is that Society will always remain one hop ahead of clerics, clerks and safety regulators. In truth the only people who seem to have recognised just what was going on were sour commentators. Thus Chaucer: 'Now as of the outrageous array of wommen, god woot that though the visages of somme of them seme ful chaast and debonaire, yet notifie they in thir array of atyr likerousnesse and pryde.' A neat dissembly, if you will. Or how about Sir Richard Maitland, writing a century and a half later:

> 'And of fine silk their furrit clokis,
> With hingan sleeves, like geil pokis;
> Nae preaching will gar them forbeir
> To weir all things that sin provokis;
> And all for newfangleness of geir.'

John Knox must have appreciated that.

107

5 GETTING THE MESSAGE

Lurking around the doings of the world there have always been those whose prime gift is communication. Painters, writers, poets, actors, dancers, singers, and the patrons of such, who are themselves in a way communicators, have been part and parcel of recorded cultures.

Their motives present a positive macédoine. They range from stark necessity – the literate slave concealed behind the stinking fur curtains of a barbarian, and able to add a few spiky comments which would never be noticed by his illiterate owner – via an extraordinary degree of brave commitment right up to the cold, commercial calculation of what is going to sell more copies of the newspaper. I confess to a problem myself in communicating a satisfactory name for this mixed salad and now that I come to think in terms of this analogy perhaps the best way is to propose the populace as the solid vegetable matter and the observers and recorders of the scenario (and those who made their work see the light of day) as a variety of dressings. The dressings can be very bland, with lots of emollient oil for Authority or Society, or they can be vinegar-sharp; they can be sweet/sour, sugary with a touch of mustard or lemon. Something healthy and naturalistic is called for from the media? A herbal dish is added. Something altogether more florid in style? Bring on the Roquefort. Sales flagging? Bring on the tomato sauce. For those quite lost as to what they suppose they are communicating I recommend the Thousand Islands dressing approach, all things to all lunch-bars.

Any culture deprived of free communication by at least one creative channel kills the spirit of man. At worst it turns man in upon himself or others of his tribe. When every form of amusement, recrea-

108

tion, expression of joy and above all enjoyment of the opposite sex is ruthlessly suppressed, the life force which must have an outlet turns brutal. Consider the fifteen years of Puritan rule in Britain. A once gallant, brave, brutal, splendid, gorgeous, merry-making nation was transformed into a society in which spying and informing on your neighbours was the only sport left (they were likely to suffer a gruesome penalty, quite possibly in public, which made up for having no theatre or church excitements) and in which the only apparent god was money. Under the Puritans, poverty became the crime which it remains to this day in several Western societies. When Charles II finally returned and the church bells were rung, that was the only music London could provide. The magical pipes and flutes and viols and lutes had been smashed, and only a few old men remained who knew how to play them.

'It is only when the artist is truly integrated into society (as he was in all the important periods of the flowering of the human spirit) that every man becomes something of an artist, that his everyday life becomes worth living, and his dress proclaims to the world, in its beauty and dignity, that he feels life to be worth living,' wrote Pearl Binder. Under Cromwell, actors were roundly whipped as rogues, and immense fines imposed on any audience unlucky enough to get caught watching a performance. The Greeks, on the other hand, used the theatre and indeed all the arts as a healthy cleansing of emotions at one remove, whether emotions of violence or sex or fantasy.

There are two distinct schools of thought about the media in Society. One is that they are no more than a mirror of what is going on anyway, the other prefers to see them in a moulding rôle. Both are true and both are false perspectives. The media, in which I include all forms of art in popular communication, do a reporting job and they also do a propaganda job, but blurring these definitions comes good old fallible human nature. Thus the media may have as many quirks as a piece of looking-glass in which some angles are always more flattering than others. Confronted with explicit instructions on what may be passed on to the public, the channels of communication sometimes unconsciously caricature themselves and their objectives, much to the delight of posterity.

What nobody can deny, though, is that if you study the media to determine their effect or non-effect upon eroticism in dress in various cultures, the only conclusion that you can come to is that they have been a deadly enemy to women. They may not have invented women as sex-objects, possibly Society did that all of its own accord, but they certainly have cemented them into that rôle. Women are almost always represented as scheming, futile, silly, the dupes of men and, above all, as men's playthings. One of the reasons that ugly

109

Twenty-five photographers gawping at two very ordinary girls; because they were topless at a time when social mores still made this the exception rather than the norm, the media were on hand to record pictures which would pull in readership. The girls are female sacrifices to male paying-power – look at the straining muscles on their necks as they try to smile.

women tend to be tiresome is that they are deeply aware of this fact. 'What do women want?' enquired the unperceptive Freud (another great enemy of women; he inculcated more complexes than he ever took away). What women wanted, in times when their lives and moneys were tightly hemmed, was to be married. But they really wanted to be married because they wanted to be bedded, to prove to Society that they measured up to the image which Society (and the media) had cast upon them. They were desirable. In modern times when women have very successful careers they still want to be bedded and a quite surprising number want to be married, if only briefly, in order to make the same point.

The media either disregards ugly women, quotes them for nuisance value (Madame de Staël), suggests that they are lesbians (Charlotte Brontë), or makes jokes at their attempts to free their appearance from being what men like by burning their brassières, even though they are highly intelligent and charming women who deserve better. Alternatively it makes fun of those such as the novelist Barbara Cartland, step-grandmother to the Princess of Wales, who make a sustained effort to look very pretty all their lives. The only ugly woman who seems to have got through was Madame de Maintenon, mistress or possibly wife of Louis XIV of France, who was by all accounts as plain as a pikestaff and a bigoted bore to boot, yet she ousted the exquisite Madame de Matignon from the King's bed. There are no records of her being invited to pose nude for an allegorical picture, or even a religious one, and positively no recorded jokes at her expense that I can find.

110

The media have almost always depicted women naked, if at all possible, or drawn attention to their clothes with very obvious suggestiveness if nudity is not possible. Look at the TV series, 'Charlie's Angels', an indictment if ever I saw one of women's progression in the real world – I used to think that no-one could damage the cause of feminism more than Doris Day or Mary Tyler Moore until I caught this latest interpretation of women as stupid, crass, but very pretty playthings for men. Can you imagine putting yourselves into the hands of a bunch of detectives (bringing women into serious life, you see) each with more teeth than a crocodile?

It amazes me that the admirable Women in Media group has not had more success in re-creating the modern rôle of women. No, now I come to think of it, I am not at all amazed. Sex-objects sell products, and for so long as women are taken by the media as sex-objects, which means that they are viewed by Society for fun and tolerated by Authority as an escape valve, so long will this go on. And what will be their erotic dress? As little as possible.

The media are also the executors of dreams and fantasies. Reportage being somewhat hard to come by in Biblical times, it has been left to later generations, and particularly to painters vaguely or actively within the Christian fold, to tell us what they thought the Biblical sex-pots looked like. Interestingly, when Hollywood came to re-enact these great sex dramas, they turned most frightfully prim. Of course Hollywood was never more than a dream itself, and the wish fulfilment of the movie-going public, and in its heyday its domination by Jewish (who hate nakedness) and Puritan (who are terrified by it) thinking made the representation of the real dance of the Seven Veils, the initial art of striptease, unacceptable. All right for Rubens, not for Susan Heywood.

It was not so to the portraitists. Bereft of the sight of female nudity as an ongoing situation, the artists take cover in the portrayal of subjects which can be justified, with a good deal of artistic licence, in a fairly lewd manner. The more covered up the day-to-day subjects, the more necessary it is for the communicator to unveil them. The harder the times, the more man needs refreshment at the expense of women. Page three of *The Sun* with its statutory nude must have done more for the morale of the unemployed in the bleak recessionary years of tight money and the tight thinking that goes with it in the 1980s than did some gory pictures of nubile female saints being tortured to death with nothing on offer to the poor of the Middle Ages. One of the most erotic pieces of sculpture ever blessed by the Church and State (though no doubt Society had a few laughs at it, as did the sculptor) is that of St Teresa by Bernini, in full and flowing fig, about to be jammed through by an arrow. The arrow being the most

111

Under the pretence of religious art, artists and sculptors have always got away with a lot of eroticism in their work. The worldly Bernini cast St Teresa in her ecstasy, supposedly religious ('I felt an angel piercing my heart with an arrow over and over again,' she wrote later) in white marble reminiscent to cynics of a public lavatory, and in a pose of voluptuous collapse more usually associated with post-coital pleasure. The arrow, Cupid's dart, is an historic phallic symbol and the fact that the good nun is totally covered up only adds excitement to this mid-seventeenth-century masterpiece.

Page Three of the *Sun* newspaper, owned by Rupert Murdoch, the Australian tycoon who bought, inter alia, the London *Times* and *Sunday Times* and the New York *Daily Post*, has become shorthand for a sexy nude picture. Readers like continuity in their paper and there is no doubt that Page Three sells extra copies. Whether it should be viewed as the exploitation of women for business purposes is questionable, since there is always a queue of young women with the right dimensions, eager to appear.

The erotic stimulus of making love fully clothed, much practised by the Indian and Japanese culture. Both woman and man are wearing three kimonos, so that arriving at the desired goal was as exciting as unpeeling an artichoke to get at the delicious heart. Just as prickly when you got there, to judge by the pictures of erotic scenes from Japan, in which the ladies' pubic hair is teased up to resemble seaweed, signifying the magical entrance to the cavern of life.

overt of phallic symbols, one can only admire the cunning of the clergy in recognising a crowd-puller when they saw one.

Since the media are on the whole keen to be popular in terms of sales, they normally represent the ideals of sexual desirability in the decade to which they cater; thus one can date what sort of style and figure has been regarded as the most attractive by different cultures, and also what people deemed as most exotic in dress at the moment critique. For instance, the great erotic Japanese drawings show the couples in layers of clothing still, and full make-up and elaborate coiffure, but then the Japanese have no natural shame of nudity. Since they are descended from the gods and have no grim conscience about original sin or Adam and Eve they regard their bodies, as did the ancient Greeks, as wondrous temples, not to be defiled with drink or drugs or over-eating, and the sexual act as a matter of the utmost delicacy and elegance.

It has to be said that women are sex-objects in Japan, too.

Where else the media has been cruel to women has been in perpetuating the concept that women must conform to an ideal in their bodily shape if they are to please men. Everyone knows teenagers who have suffered everything from anorexia nervosa to being just plain farouche because they are certain in their hearts that their shape is not pleasing. Why won't your daughter take off her jacket, even when it's boiling hot? She fears that her breasts are too big, or too small. British women particularly spend their adolescence stooping to hide the growth and end up with round shoulders before their time. However, since they also hunch to hide a lack of the bust which the media have told them is essential I would advocate jackets with no questions asked in place of a later spinal disability.

The misrepresentation, or more truly the maltreatment, of women by the media has been going on for a very long time. Consider how women figure in the Old Testament. Susanna, rash enough to say 'no' to a couple of nasty old lechers who fancied her, was accused of fornication and condemned to death out of spite, only being rescued in the nick of time by young Daniel with a smart legal point. Bathsheba was the sex-object of David, and if, as depicted by the school of Antwerp in c. 1520, she really did go bathing in full view of the palace clad only in a choice number of baubles and with a running water system ejaculated from the member of the figure atop the fountain, she was rather over-reacting to her rôle, one feels. Jewels and nakedness are a very sexy combination, as Josephine Baker, the stunning negress cabaret star, was to prove a couple of thousand years later. On Bathsheba they incited a murder.

Then there is Delilah, whom I envisage as terribly pretty, terribly stupid and very grasping. She was used as a spy by her male compatriots and was so moulded in her subservient female rôle that she was quite complaisant in sending her lover to a hideous fate, nasty little beast. Salome was a political toy, used by her mother to retain the affection of her step-father so that he would give her the murder of a political prisoner who was most dangerous to her corrupt and immoral lifestyle; the Baptist, who was a communicator in a big way, had seen fit to point out to the public the errors of her ways. The media have their martyrs.

Precisely the opposite obtains for men. While women have been stripped literally, spiritually or mentally by the media whenever possible or if dressed, dressed whenever possible in the most blatantly erotic clothes; when a woman on trial for the murder of her lover's wife can find double-page spreads in the tabloid press devoted not to what she has done but to what she has worn to her trial, with choice details of cut and colour, men have worked the media very much to their own advantage. In so doing they have also not lost one jot of their attraction to the opposite sex, for clever men are always portrayed in garb which exemplifies their own special power. Women have got lumbered with having to be 'beautiful'; men, the ruler, have plumped for that other most erotic symbol, power.

In a way, it makes a very neat compromise, for in showing their power through dress men are only extending the same principle of virility and the ability to procreate which is inherent in priapic statues, whose personal equipment has been rendered by the artists in truly daunting proportions. Not everyone is perfect. Not every man gets to be king or chairman or pop idol, but then not everyone was invited to model for a fertility statue either, one suspects.

On at least one occasion, though, the media have shown themselves the true friend of both sexes. I refer to their thinking up the cunning wheeze of Courtly Love, one of the great whitewashing jobs of all time.

114

Courtly Love was celebrated in song, verse, prose, in pictures and in homilies. What it boiled down to was this: in Western Europe of medieval times there tended to be a lot of parfit gentil knights either off misappropriating the chattels and lands of other p.g.k.s who might or might not be foreign (or even dusky), or off stewing like lobsters in their unsuitable armour to fight non-p.g.k.s who had turned out to be on the wrong side of God (these were even more likely to be dusky). Either way, it meant a long absence from the boudoir of the little woman left in charge at home. Since these establishments tended to be the same size as an average village there was a sporting chance that lurking among the hangers-on to the lordly table would be a media man. No bad thing, probably. He would be able to turn out a neat poem or a funny article, to sing or to play, and thus to while away the incredibly tedious hours of the ladies while their lords were away, none knew when to return (until the ransom note arrived). There have after all always been more writers commenting from the home front than there have been providing 'dispatches from hell before breakfast'. Also creative persons tend to be, well, of a courtly disposition.

However, also lurking within this extended family were the sons of other wealthy families, pages, knights errant, passers-by who dropped in for years, in short a seething mass of highly sexed, potent young men – and all alone with one's wife. Even those noble lords who were better with the broadsword and the mace than with witty, delicate conversation must sometimes have wondered what was going on.

No need. By every intermittent post from his favourite troubadour, chamberlain or what-have-you, he was assured that while the entire establishment had spent the night in the woods or gone on a four-day picnic, they had been listening to the sweet song of the nightingale or recording the wonders of nature in their breviaries. Modern newspapers would call it the tease of all time. One has only to look at the pictures of that date. There they all are, young, lusty, dressed to the nines, panting with unfulfilled desire, fit to be tied by the erotic dress of their neighbours. And all passion apparently diverted into innocent worship from afar.

Even more of a whitewash job was done by the media (subsequently) on what have come to be regarded as fairy stories. Our generation thinks of the Sleeping Princess, Snow White, and Cinderella. As the Sleeping Princess was originally written (in Perceforest and Pentamarone) the handsome prince turned up, fell in love with what he saw, raped her and left (for the wars?). Charles Perrault in 1697 was much kinder. He had the loving kiss and a happy union to offer. Much the same scenario applies to Snow White, equally an

115

heiress worth fighting over (the seven dwarfs were the precursors of the Gnomes of Zurich, perhaps) and as for Cinderella – well, that is a real foot-fetish story. A mistake changed the slipper to glass. In Perrault's original version it was 'pantoufle en vair' (a slipper of fur) but being hand-copied, it came out as a pantoufle en verre, glass.

Perrault must have known perfectly well the eroticism associated with a fur-trimmed slipper. The perfect fit meant the perfect vagina to please her husband. What Walt Disney would have thought is best left to the imagination. None had more imagination than he, and in a way his constant symbolism of exquisite innocence protected by anthropomorphised animals who would never harm her might be thought by some to have a relationship, by a leap of the imagination I admit, with the rescue of the maiden Andromeda by Perseus, far closer than the allegorical rape of territory implicit certainly in Sleeping Beauty. Andromeda is unclothed, Snow White has little puff-sleeves which have gone into the lexicon of fashion. Each touches a chord in the heart of man, the hunter.

Hard as one might try in view of the plethora of recent books on the

The appeal of this 1981 image (left) is that of Snow White, the Sleeping Beauty, Cinderella – vulnerable innocence, limpid eyes, tousled hair, white frills and a big, girlish bow. Some day her prince will come, for sure. The intensely romantic, faun-like fairy-tale heroine gets the rabbits, real and human, to do the washing-up.

Right: Never mind the accuracy, get the sexy message. Never mind if Henry VIII is made to eat tomatoes or Robin Hood to smoke a Havana, never mind that Errol Flynn in the epic movie *Captain Blood* (1935), was dressed in a costume dating from 200 years before that of his love, Olivia de Havilland. It's the spark that counts. Nobody seeing this early version of *Cleopatra* could have cared less that Egyptians never wore pearls, which were so rare and costly in that part of the world, coming as they did from the Orient, that they were incalculable treasures. With such devices, and with displays of ornate splendour in costume as in all its settings, Hollywood in its early years brought the dreams of the drab to life, and clerks went home visualising themselves in Roman armour.

The movie *His Girl Friday* (1940) showed a woman for the first time really competing for a man's job, and beating him to the deadline as well. What she wore to accomplish this feat was a straight adaptation by Robert Kalloch of the working man's outfit, even to the hat, though given some special curves. The joke played on the chalk-stripe suit, which ends up with all the lines running to point up the breasts and to demonstrate the fact that she is definitely bifurcated, is worthy of Givenchy and his zebra print on the second colour plate following page 48.

subject, no one could make a study of erotic dress without including Hollywood. In fact they should not try at all hard for lurking among the costume credits for everything from the dignified to the dingy is as comprehensive a catalogue of what turns on the cross-sectioned public as ever you will find in the other media. Newspapers in the main need to be specific in what they provide if they are to be profitable (readers like continuity). In Hollywood, on the other hand, upon a mere few thousand acres of film lots, were encapsulated the wildest dreams of everyone, actors themselves included, of eroticism in dress.

Snow White to Rita Hayworth, innocence to blatancy; every taste is catered for, for that is precisely what movies in their heyday were about, escapism and dreams. That the clothes horses whose lovely visages ended inevitably happy did not know Shakespeare from Hemingway mattered not in the least. Nor did most of the goggling audience. Who remembers the brilliant script and the wisecracks in *To Have and to Have Not* now? What they remember is a rake-thin Lauren Bacall managing to show an awful lot of curves and indentations while wearing what appeared to be a conventional tailored suit. Not for the gogglers, the stenographers who were never going to need a ball gown or a lot of ostrich feather fans in anything other than their dream lives, to worry or to note that the cutting of Miss Bacall's suit in that film could be accounted one of the highest achievements of couture. But the tailored suit you find again in *His Girl Friday*, as worn by Rosalind Russell as the new breed of emancipated woman – presaging a war? Certainly boding no good for male dominance,

118

although, pin-stripes notwithstanding, she is ultimately submissive – to the better dressed man in her life. Indeed, the victor for her only half-liberated mind dismisses his rival with kindly enquiries as to whether, since he is carrying an umbrella, he is also wearing galoshes? Yes, he is. What more need be said about this fellow, garbed not in the Authority of a double-breasted suit, but cowering from the elements and so not heroic. The fact that he is a thoroughly nice man counts for nought as the heroine assesses the virility of her mate; he may be dangerous (any one of us could have told her that he would clear off next day) but oh, the scent of power and danger.

I have deliberately used this illustration of eroticism in film costume because it seems to me to be one that has been ignored by social historians, and since sex is the life-blood of Society it is a gap which needs filling. For in introducing the new breed of woman *before* World War II the costumiers were reacting unconsciously to changes in Society which were only just beginning to show their heads. Instead of following well-trodden paths of proven symbols of sexual dress, this section of the media actually set a trend which was extended beyond fantasy into everyday life. Not for nothing did Gilbert Adrian, exemplar of the woman-cut suit, move on to become a main-line name in general-store merchandise too.

Dance, of course, can claim a place in erotic dress on several fronts. In the Cause of Art (note the capitals) practically anything is acceptable provided you can get it past the Hays Office, the Lord Chamberlain and the coach-tour traffic. Dance is much more wicked than theatre. Theatre is either a perfect reflection of socially acceptable fashion (Jack Buchanan breaks new ground by wearing a double-breasted jacket on stage – heavens, will the skies fall?) or it is deliberately blatant (striptease: posed nudes moving on to moving nudes). Ballet has a slightly broader appeal: naughtiness – Isadora Duncan showing her feet, and diaphanously draped around a liberated and somewhat freely available torso, the complete opposite of the dancers of the opera-ballet who were so tightly laced that one felt it a positive duty, having delivered the roses, to undo those constricting tu-tus and relieve the tiny, panting frame, so exhausted from that pas de deux when he would tread on her toe and, because of the costume, was able, in the Cause of Art, to place his hands in some extremely personal areas whilst murmuring, 'I'll drop you, you cow, if you don't stop upstaging me.' Oh well, the sexual duel of the stage.

In media terms the true inheritor of Hollywood must be the advertising business when one comes to erotic dress. This is because only advertising has also succeeded on the mass scale in using erotic dress to cater to each and every taste, and has used women and their physical attributes to sell everything from dreams to refrigerators.

119

Naturally, as with the dreams of the silver screen, dress has played an enormous part. Just as Hollywood managed to capitalise on eroticism in dress, so too has advertising managed to peddle every kind of sex in every kind of dress to the profit of its clients, as the pictures which close this chapter show.

Did you know that a strapless dress, arm bangles, a tight neckband and rosettes in your hair were a great help in getting the gas cylinder to provide a lumière réglèe, or adjustable light (above left)? Possibly not. Join the crowd which was equally astonished though equally charmed by the sales tactics of Cycles A. Mercier (above right), whose heroine, should she have ventured onto the boulevards in that degree of décolletage, must surely have brought the rue de Birague, to say nothing of the rest of Paris, to a halt. It is a bicycle for a man, by the way, and in her other hand the Amazon sports an oversize butterfly to emphasise the lightness of the machine. This is advertising at its most obvious and sexy — even the skirt is swept in between the thighs. As for the Argyll socks. . . .

It's that lift and separate, hand behind the head and legs ahoy look again, this time pushing motor cars (far left) and the sort of clothes you should wear if you want to get a girl like that into your family saloon (left).

Elliott
atent
skin
tight
white

...and scarlet, black or horrid beige **10 gns** at all shops

Above: The advertising poster most smeared with stickers saying 'This exploits women' on the escalators of the London Underground railway. It is hardly subtle, but the application of 'horrid' to beige, that safest of all colours, at least gives a hint of humour.

If you thought erotic dress was a strange way to sell gas-cylinders, bicycles and motor cars, stick around for this attempt (right) by the use of nudity to promote a cigarette lighter. It will hang on the walls of a thousand tobacconists.

HIGHLIGHT

October 1982

feudor Lighters

Mon		4	11	18	25
Tues		5	12	19	26
Wed		6	13	20	27
Thur		7	14	21	28
Fri	1	8	15	22	29
Sat	2	9	16	23	30
Sun	3	10	17	24	31

6 SHARED SECRETS

A<small>S SOON</small> as you mention the subject of erotic dress the eyes of men light up and the eyes of women glaze over, and for the same reason. Both sexes immediately assume that you are talking about female underwear, which is a subject for dreams and fantasies for men and a subject not quite nice to mention in public for women. Men think that you are talking about bunny girls in evening-dress corsets, or black silk knickers, or striptease dancers, or Bette Midler; so do women.

Yet the great novelist Balzac, who died in 1850, noted that only a fool or a philospher would go into his wife's dressing-room. Had he lived another hundred years he would have witnessed the unacceptable props and stays of womanhood, the gadgets to which she resorted in order to keep up her outward finery, transformed into a quite unnecessary and therefore delectable design object to be worshipped as a fetish and worn for intense pleasure. By 1977 French knickers were being sold even in Marks and Spencer of all places, largest purveyors of undies to the British. They were draughty and inconvenient – you had to buy a suspender belt, which M and S steadfastly refused to supply, and stockings in place of those handy tights which at least kept everything else from falling down or out – but feminine. Under all those layers and layers which fashion decreed, after fifteen years of sexless tights, the self-satisfaction of the secret dress had arrived.

It is not hard to understand why. As women have progressed into the once male-dominated world so they too have become subject to the drab conformity which merits promotion. When Margaret Thatcher became Prime Minister of Great Britain in 1979 she chose

per Gavarni A.D.

Ah! par exemple! voilà qui est bizarre!... ce matin j'ai fait un nœud à .... la et ce soir il y a une rosette!...

her dress image with as much care as her cabinet. The image she selected was tailored, calm, authoritative, and all the softening pussy-cat bows in the world could not prevent her being labelled an iron lady. She was in effect wearing the dress of powerful men since the Industrial Revolution and as a prime product of the work-ethic oriented class which was bred under Cromwell, it was perfectly appropriate. However, the lady obviously does have another side to her since on occasions she has slipped into something quite superbly flattering and very exotic by the designer Yuki, whose skill is to leave everything to the imagination in draped dresses which one moment hide, the next offer a peep of, the inner woman. Of all the British designers he is the most sensuous to the wearer. So does the Prime Minister, who is an extremely pretty, blonde woman with a mind as formidable as a tank, perhaps wear silken lingerie under all that navy gabardine? As she dismisses ministers, humbles our foes, charms the necessary and goes about her business demure in dress as a nun, is she underneath a froth of Janet Reger? And wouldn't you like to know?

Of course you would, because the whole erotic impulse of underwear is that of secrecy, of intimacy, of knowing something the others do not. It is privileged information for your eyes only, and the double-take is that of all erotic dress except perhaps transvestitism, it is equally erotic to the wearer as to the lucky partner.

Greta Garbo is always said to have insisted, under the plainest

Above left: 'How extraordinary! This morning I tied a knot and this evening there is a bow.' The husband, privileged, as he thinks, alone to enjoy the charms of his wife's uncorseted body, is baffled by the change in the lacing of the instrument of her submission to his masculine taste. If love can laugh at locksmiths, it can certainly laugh at short-sighted, gullible husbands.

Above right: A visual encapsulation of the ridiculous lengths to which male-dominated Society will demand that women go in order to present an attractive silhouette. One cannot help being moved by the vulnerable yet resigned expression on the face of the young girl as she sits, surrounded by crinoline hoops which suggest that her eventual appearance will owe more to the art of the civil engineer than to that of the dress designer.

123

For 27/6 (£1.37½ or about $2.57) in 1901 you could have your dream of comfort in the Specialité Corset. There was no need to slip into a loose tea-gown to relieve the pressure on your guts. Tucked up on her deep, buttoned Chesterfield, the lady certainly looks relaxed, possibly because she knows that at any moment an admirer will whisk through the door and take the beastly thing off.

clothes, that her lingerie be made of pure silk. 'Why?' protested the studio, 'no one's going to see it. It's terribly expensive and no one's going to know it's silk.'

'I shall know,' retorted the star, 'and I shall walk differently.'

Balzac should have been living in this age of industrial espionage, then he could have said that only a fool, a philosopher or somebody who wanted to find out something very important about a woman would go into her dressing-room. Were I employed upon such business, I should forget all those expensive bugging devices and clambering around at unsocial hours, and just head for the lingerie drawer. This would apply whether I were trying to snare either a powerful woman herself, and there are some around, or more likely still to snare the man in her life, for her choice would tell you a lot about him, too, and therefore how he's likely to be vulnerable. Private 'tecs hired to follow suspected spouses should equally stop running up huge expenses in the smart restaurants of the world in observing têtes-à-têtes in which the conversation between ladies and gentlemen who are not married one to another is less likely to be of the 'Darleeng, be mine' genre than of who can get out their American Express card quicker at the end. Tea at the Ritz in the 1980s, it seems, means just that.

So the private 'tec should abandon the quails (again?) and head for the lady's lingerie drawer. This will tell him everything he needs to tell his client. We all know that the first rumblings of many divorces are the discovery in some inner pocket or carelessly left file of overseas hotel expenses which, funnily enough, seem to be for two persons. But when is somebody going to compile a list of initial rumblings caused by hubby noticing in his wife's half-unpacked bag a terribly saucy little piece of nightwear which he quite certainly does not

124

remember as gracing the nuptial couch, to which she is prone to come in flaccid brushed nylon.

The closer to the bone, the sweeter tastes the flesh. The closer to the body, the more delicious the savour of the dress. The ultimate erotic appeal of lingerie is that of intimacy. It is therefore not surprising that lingerie, in the way that we think of it – i.e. the eyes lighting up or glazing over – is a comparatively novel thing. Only as women have moved further into the territory once dominated by men, and in doing so adopted considerable areas of their clothing, has under-clothing been a cause of excitement. There are still older gentlemen alive who remember aunts born in the mid-nineteenth century who were mortified by not being allowed to wear knickers, which were considered indecent, the implication being that you were so far removed from delicacy as to be likely to reveal more than you ought in playing, romping or going on the licentious swing. The aunts thought it would have been much more fun to wear knickers and to hell with falling over.

So with woman wrapped in the garb of business, woman at war, woman climbing the professional ladders, her outward dress became in many instances as conformist as that of her male counterpart. But it took until the 'sixties, with 'dress for yourself or your lover' as the only diktat standing among the ruins of Paris says . . ., *Vogue* says . . ., that lingerie became a priority for the masses, not the mistresses.

Plain clothes made plain women plainer still. Stark separates, classic, boring, 'safe' clothes heralded the economic collapse and crise de nerfs among the designers. For the few, who live a life and have a bank balance to support exquisite fantasy dresses from Bill Gibb and Zandra Rhodes, it is all right; by day a grub, by evening a butterfly. Jeans and chiffon, and not too much worry about what goes under either. But for a whole other section of women, lingerie has taken off. It is so attractive that a lot of pretty women buy it too, but when you ask them about it they shrug and say, yes, we have tons of it, but we never wear it because quite simply nobody sees it – if the man is attracted he doesn't want to mess about admiring your Chantilly lace inserts, he wants to get the whole damn' lot off as fast as possible.

'A woman would be in despair if nature had formed her as fashion makes her appear,' remarked Mlle de Lespinasse. Leaving aside deliberate mutilation or cosmetic surgery, the easiest way to appear as fashion dictates at any time is to wear something underneath the outer covering which will substantially alter the shape of the body as viewed by the outside world. To this end have rolls and pads been added through the ages, hoops and half-hoops and contraptions like bird-cages stuffed underneath the flimsiest gowns, or alternatively

How this elaborate underwear fitted beneath the sheer, short, shift dresses of the 1920s is hard to work out, though psychologically it is right in line with the theory that the more boring the outer layer, the more sexy the underneath has to be. This was true again in the Great Knicker Revival of the mid-1970s.

125

Known as the whirlpool bra, this hideous contraption (right) supported the still bust-conscious 1950s. So did the equally off-putting girdle in 'power net'. Its full horror was supplanted only by the pantie girdle, also in power net and especially horrid when extended to thigh length.

Below: Idealised undies. This pouter-pigeon-breasted beauty is from an American calendar of the late 1940s though what she was selling is lost to record. Dog food? Unlikely though it may seem, God, or Jehovah, may be considered the inventor of knickers. Amid a plethora of instructions to Moses recorded in the book of Exodus is a detailed clothes list for Aaron, the High Priest, of which the final item is linen breeches which must reach from loin to thigh.

iron, wood, whalebone or elastomeric fibre used to control and pare down the contours of the figure. Of course the de Lespinasse quote may be read in two ways; one is that the lady found the fashion of her time (she lived in the middle years of the eighteenth century) dull and unflattering. The evocation of that period which will probably come readiest to the mind of readers is the work of the artist Hogarth, a supreme commentator on Society's activities who quite rightly for his genre missed not one button nor one curve in portraying his subjects. Thus any woman who actually looked like this naturally must be in despair. But this is not the interpretation most would place on the words. Most would assume that the spiky French lady was pointing out an eternal fashion truth, which is that at least half the fun of dressing up resides in the complications of changing oneself to the proper mould required by Society.

Even the Greeks, so long held up as the master protagonists of 'natural' dress, which supposes no artifice in achieving by under-pinnings invisible the outward and manifest shape of allure, wore breast supporters or repressors which must have been most uncomfortable. Called fasciae, these precursors of the 1920s desire to be both bosomless and loosely clothed could only be called seductive by a partner who had been living in an unenlightened monastery. They were, simply, bandages. Swaddling clothes at birth and, had Plato had his way, up to the age of two were the order of the Greek day. Youthful, burgeoning womanhood and the sagging contours of mid-life were to be equally restricted. In many cultures the dead were as

126

carefully wrapped up as a Havana cigar. It could be cradle to grave in fasciae.

Similarly, it is a little hard to equate those remorselessly padded, underwired, cantilevered props and stays of the outer form, which continued until everyone let everything hang out in the 1970s, with eroticism. Could anything truly be less romantic than a pair of elasticated trunks 'with thigh control' in a fearful white which soon went grey or showed signs of distress after much washing. Secrets they maybe were, intimate they certainly were, but they were neither secrets to be shared not an intimacy which begged participation.

On the other hand much of what people think of as underwear does not fit into this chapter because it is blatantly directed: straps and suspenders, garters and bindings, corsets and lacings, strict wiring and a lot of metal fastenings are not for an essay on intimacy. They fit in the case of corsets into the considerations put forward under Society, and in the case of those extraordinary arrangements of thin bonds of fabric which criss-cross the torso like an electricity grid, well, they are attractive to the mind which admires discipline in clothing, and at any rate are now so well exposed as to constitute a deliberate costume. Bette Midler, the Lido in Paris, countless advertisements and countless sleazy clubs have turned this sort of underwear into outerwear. With this transformation disappears the thrill of intimacy.

Lingerie for lingerie's sake. In 1974 the return of an impractical if not downright inconvenient garment, the cami-knicker, heralded new thinking in Society's pursuit of erotic dress. Outwardly, clothes were placid and woolly, which men hated, and such tantalising lacy extravagances as this had been relegated by the feminist movement to the preserve of tarts and mistresses. However, due largely to the foresight of designer Janet Reger, an item of skin-to-skin wear which had been created to be worn under brief dresses and with stockings held up by garters, and which looked unlikely, to say the least, with the 1970s tights or even the re-born suspender belt, emerged as a high fashion item. Not only high fashion: the cami-knicker filtered through to the chain stores too where, with devastating practicality and a surely unintentional erotic effect, the manufacturers fitted three tiny buttons at the crotch.

The undergarment I suspect readers would most associate with eroticism (after knickers) is the corset. The problem is that the corset is such a complex garment and operates on so many different levels that it really ought to get a mention in every single chapter of a book such as this. For starters, it has obvious bondage and submission symbolism, frequently to the extent of danger. Then it defies Authority when Society laces itself to fainting pitch and wrecks its rib-cages and liver, despite the pleas of the medical profession, in order to be 'attractive' and thus snare a mate. It is an economic pointer – Veblen described it as in economic theory an object of mutilation for the purposes of lowering the subject's vitality and rendering her obviously unfit for work. On the other hand, Authority approved the corset because it suppressed lustful feeling (what with wondering if you were going to be sick) and lust-inducing curves, until Society in its determination to cock a snook turned it into a flagrant manipulation of the shape of the dress over it. But it was – is – essentially in my view a prop and stay of an outward and visible form, and was not intended to be discovered, however gratifying it may have been to the wearer to know that the cause of her agony was covered in pretty lace. All corset advertising is directed at the ultimate wearer, unlike advertisements for lingerie which have much more the tenor of gifts to be exchanged between lovers.

Indeed, so dull and unsightly was modern underwear considered until recently that older ladies had a long, low stool at the ends of their beds upon which elastomeric control garments and prosaic celanese directoire knickers were laid to rest at night, covered with a discreet special cloth. Far from being erotic, in one famous divorce case in the 'twenties the wife cited as yet another instance of her husband's brutality that he had 'laughed at her couvre-linge'. What a simply beastly thing to do, what a cad he must have been.

But the corset has no true place in a section which examines one of our premises for erotic dress, intimacy. The pure silk satin lining of an outwardly staid evening gown is more erotic in this context. It will also have been noted by now that men scarcely figure in this rustle through the privacy of dress. The reason is quite plain. Men have not worn distorting underwear, save for the corset, but have relied for their outward bodily shape on pads and puffs built into their clothes which, far from being erotic in the discovery, have throughout history been a source of embarrassment. There is an enchanting story of a handsome soldier, one Coignet, who came into Paris in 1809 with Napoleon's army and, being a solid fellow, got promoted to the rank of sergeant at a pay rise to 43 sous per day. But with promotion went, as always save in the case of harlots, responsibility. He had to learn to write and he had to wear silk stockings.

128

Right: Samson and Delilah by Van Dyck. Every age relies to a large extent on its media (which until recently meant primarily its painters) to establish its ideals of beauty and eroticism in clothing, and in painting yet again the story of this great sex symbol, Van Dyck treated her as a contemporary allegory clad in topical costume. This gruesome tale is responsible for the hair complexes of a million men, but must have given a terrific boost to the sale of toupees.

Below: Something to please everyone, even a millionaire: Monroe all curves as usual, Betty Grable with a bust aimed for moonshots and just as armoured as a rocket, and Lauren Bacall dressed to appeal to bachelors of delicate sensibilities with domineering mothers. This still from *How to Marry a Millionaire* is a classic of Hollywood type-dressing.

Erotic dress in advertising. The photograph above was used in an advertisement for De Beers diamonds, and the suggestion is that if you buy the girl a very expensive piece of jewellery, she will grant you certain privileges. The use of the hat; fashionably quite out of place with the dress, is interesting because the concealment of the hair and the veiling of the face reinforce the sense of possession which money can buy. It is the dress of acquiescence too, but this woman knows that.

A fashion advertisement (right) which ruffled the feathers of the women's liberation faction. They should not have worried because the message is so unsubtle that short of hitting the prospective customer over the head with a sledge-hammer, the point could hardly be banged home more firmly. The piquant aspect is that the advertisers, Dormeuil, are the infinitely respectable producers of high-priced men's suitings, and if you can afford high-priced suitings then surely you must have learned to upgrade your taste, at any rate in public, from girls dressed like hostesses in a Shanghai massage parlour. Does this ad-man's fantasy, an almost naked girl on a pedestal, suggest that womanhood is still sacred? Or what?

By 1919 corset manufacturers were in despair, and Mrs Caresse Crosby's invention of a brassière designed to support the breasts, though patented in 1914, was still a gleam in the eye of hopeful males. So lingerie, which had previously been so hideous that it had to be covered with a frilly camisole, or hidden from sight by a couvre-linge, suddenly got to be pretty. Madonna lilies and billets doux could be confidently expected by any woman wearing pink silk crêpe de Chine underpinnings, since a lot of the dresses, though beaded, were very sheer and very heavy. It made sense, especially when those underpinnings were decorated with embroidery in the same style as the tiny tokens of affection that she could presumably also expect via jewellers Boucheron or Cartier.

Since the art of merchandising dress is largely persuading people that they need things that they do not need, it follows that once corsets were an essential part of the wardrobe, one was simply not enough. There must be corsets to go under every different shape of dress, and also to suit the mood of the occasion. This charming lady of 1830 must have been a trendsetter since the gradual restriction of the flowing Regency dresses had begun only a year or two previously. She signals the social and physical bondage of women for the next seventy years.

Figures speak louder than words

Model your figure with a
Model
brassière

Beautiful Style Catalogue sent free on request

Model Brassière Co.
200 Fifth Avenue, New York

The trouble with the underwear manufacturers is that their products, even when as pretty as these, do tend to be in the wrong place at the wrong time. About the least erotic item of dress must be the bra-strap, particularly if it is greyish-white and slightly sagging. British women are notorious for their cardigans and their bra-straps and if you look at the picture opposite you can hazard a reason for the latter. In showing a very pretty, flattering lingerie set, the promoters of the product have also chosen to show the dress designed to be worn over it. Now, the dress has a low V-neck and V-back, narrow shoulder straps which obviously sit at mid-point, and an armhole which looks to be quite cut away. Under this the heroine is apparently proposing to wear a bra designed for a dress with a high back, low cleavage and tight armhole or sleeves.

Lingerie for display and for blatant sex appeal (right) – not functional, practical or designed to be worn out of sight.

Political underwear (below), chosen to please the man who is paying the bill. The pretty French girl of 1899 wears red for visits by her Socialist admirer; red, white and blue, the tricolor shades, for her Nationalist parliamentarian friend; a print of fleur-de-lys, the French emblem before the Revolution, for her Royalist lover; but for the Anarchist – nothing.

DESSOUS POLITIQUES

Quand elle reçoit son protecteur socialiste, elle met des dessous rouges...

Quand arrive son député nationaliste, elle met des dessous tricolores...

Pour celui de la « Jeunesse royaliste », dessous fleurdelisés...

Pour l'anarchiste, elle met... la peau!...

Dessin de Gil Baer.

Classic eroticism in dress (left). A marvellously styled picture from *Harpers & Queen* in 1980 which presents woman as valuable prey – if you can catch her. Lured by the innate desire to touch her magnificent and shiny pelt and to get to grips with this foxy lady, the predatory male who is successful finds out that it is fox-fur to female skin at one pounce. He is further enchanted by the innocence of her teenager-style little gestures to modesty (Elvis Presley was mad about girls in simple white panties).

Colour has a sexuality of its own, with black and red the favourite colours by far in the male mind. Above is a classic vision of the scarlet woman, while black also suggests naughty possibilities, however elegant the ensemble. The least stimulating colours for dress are dark brown and grey, though both are immensely flattering to the Nordic complexion. Olive-skinned Latins can get away with citrus-fruit colours, but then Latins can get away with practically anything.

Swiss national costume, the perfect blend of peasant practicality and age-old sexual signalling. The big sleeves of the blouse suggest good working potential underneath but also a fine décolletage when the snow melts, or rather when she melts and the gaily patterned fichu can be removed. Though well braced in her corselet for the rigours of the day, nevertheless her lacings – supporting the breasts, narrowing the waist and ending in a dinky bow which hangs over her pudenda – suggest an invitation to unlace which could go on till the cows come home.

For those of quick decision there is no fastening more alluring than the press-stud, the more obvious the better. Studs require no tedious unbuttoning or unlacing, they pose no hint of resistance; on the contrary, they invite you to take the two halves in your bare hands and let rip. Odds are that the guy in this picture never got to make his 'phone call, especially since he is wearing a zip and poppers too.

Unfortunately his spindly nether limbs had hitherto been warmly concealed because he came from the sans-culotte class – one should remember that sans-culotte does not actually mean without trousers, or drawers of some sort; it means unable to afford proper trousers, i.e. knee-breeches, those symbols of aristocracy and Authority because they exposed the thoroughbred calf completed by the exquisite ankle and the high-instepped foot, all the signs of power and leisure. Now Sergeant Coignet had neither power, leisure, nor an inclination, it seems, for the dress expected of him on his 43 sous per day. However, since he was a bright man, and incidentally a perfect example of the necessary power of dress in elevating oneself in Society, he accepted that to be calfless among the grand set at his captain's table was to be a failure in the boudoir. He therefore purchased false calves, perhaps not knowing that he was doing no more than his superiors had been doing for ages, though only their valets would know.

The effect was all that he could have anticipated. The handsome sergeant found himself, false calves and all, between two lovely women, très chic, who vied for his company to be continued in their

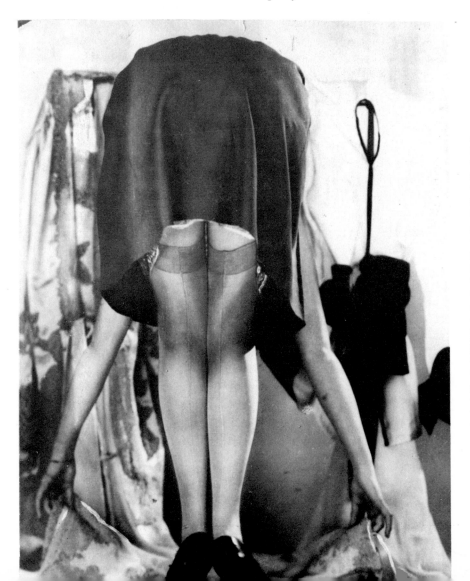

Art overcomes the risks of exposure. This dainty-fingered window-dresser in the West End of London provided passers-by with a quite surprising erotic shock. A substantial backside is hoisted at a most tempting angle and reveals a glimpse of bare thigh, panties above and the dragon stocking-tops below. The seams on the stockings are in themselves a turn-on, shaping the calf and leading the eye upward, but the posture of the feet, with the insteps collapsed to help her reach down to the floor and the practical spreading out of the feet for balance, suggest to the wary male that when she stands up this lady may not be in first youth and may also be liable to give a cheeky fellow a clout on the ear.

beds. Settling on the more possessive one, he whisked round to her mansion, but instead of having a simply lovely time romping about the bedchamber, all he was worried about was where to hide the blasted leggings when they got into bed. In the end he hid them under the pillows, which made it all very uncomfortable, and in the morning – presumably he had proved inadequate, quite apart from the spindleshanks – madame tactfully left him to dress alone (was she Madame Balzac?) but made it a strictly one-night stand.

The Puritans had texts from the Bible embroidered on their undies, which must have been a real turn-off. 'Thou, God, see-est all' is calculated to freeze the warmest parts, especially if not absolutely the most stunningly proportioned.

There is an area, though, wherein men feature as objects of erotic intimacy. Strangely perhaps, it is in the area of jewellery. Once the overt symbol of status, jewellery is now the staid dress of the company chairman, or even more likely the id-soothing underwear of the beautiful man who must rest for a while in the shadow of Authority. Those clearly out of the closet wear their shirts open to the navel and loads of gold and turquoise, with diamond ear-rings in one pierced ear only. Ted Tinling, the famous tenniswear designer, had a terrible hassle with Harrods, who refused to pierce him. 'We don't do gentlemen,' they said. 'What makes you think I am a gentleman?' retorted the six-foot-seven, septuagenarian, gallant ex-colonel.

But this is not to do with intimacy, this is to do with power and Authority. Intimacy in jewellery is the discovery that under the Turnbull and Asser shirt there is a slim gold chain. Really predatory females prefer the chain to have a religious symbol on it, so that they know that they are getting the man away not only from his wife but from his religion also.

There is also the extremely sensuous tactility of gold, either superfine or barbarically thick, against the naked skin. It is six o'clock in the morning, and already the sun is chinking through my curtains, softly grey-gold across the white bed. My left arm is stretched outside the covers, reaching down to caress the head of my cat. She stretches, yawns, curls her tail, folds her toes under in submissive position preparatory to nipping my wrist. I stretch, yawn and look along my arm, and there, just catching the light as I turn my wrist, is a hint of gold. Hair-fine, demolishable it would seem by a pat from a pussy paw, protected by the magic of its metal, a secret jewel. Within minutes it will vanish under a sleeve, under a watch of solid proportions which is going to tell me that I am late for my prosaic duties, by the evening beneath something more appropriately splendid for the party game. But just now, and indeed always, I find it the most personally erotic piece of jewellery I own, because nobody but myself, or those privileged to know about it, know that it is there.

An aspect of erotic dress, or maybe undress, which I have found difficult to incorporate – no apologies for the pun – into this book has been the question of bodily mutilation, those fleshly pin-tuckings in particular which are now found only among the most primitive of tribes or on the most sophisticated handbags. They hover between the fetish of tactility, the stamps of Authority, Society's signalling system, and the mark of heroes.

In the end, I have chosen to put them into this chapter about underwear and intimacy because it seems to me that while tattoos, paint, nipple-piercing, pain, inconvenience and status symbols will be perfectly obvious in the context of, say, Authority or indeed may come under practically any of the eight major areas of eroticism in dress dealt with in this book, it is the area of intimacy which is the most cogent.

For body-scoring, as opposed to body-painting, suggests the ultimate privilege of intimacy, of being permitted to touch, to caress, to hold, to possess. For the woman, body-scoring is the primitive equivalent of the corset, of constrictive underwear, because it implies suffering in the cause of exciting the male. Interestingly, in view of the observations already made about the preferences of position for sexual enjoyment implied by dress and by stance, body-scoring upon the woman equally suggests a preference for the position of coitus. The most common patterns, which look to blasé Western eyes somewhere between an Arran knitting pattern for a sweater and one of those doormats woven by sex-starved sailors on trips to humid climes, are to be found on the backs of the women and the chests of the men. Little sensory stimulation could thus have been enjoyed had the couples adopted the 'missionary' approach. Tactility is the erotic aspect of body-scoring, and it is as an arousal by intimacy that it is mentioned here.

Touch here to conquer

'Where's the man can ease a heart like a satin gown?' queried Dorothy Parker. Where, indeed. So free a spirit, she dismissed boring fabrics beloved by Dr Jaeger and the reformists and went, as a customer, for satin. 'Satin's for the free.'

Hers is an interesting personal statement from the wearer's point of view, but there is no doubt that the colour, the feel and the smell of the fabrics from which clothes are made is enormously erotic; and as always, there must be taken into consideration the effect upon the observer.

Twice in my life I have been asked by almost complete strangers in

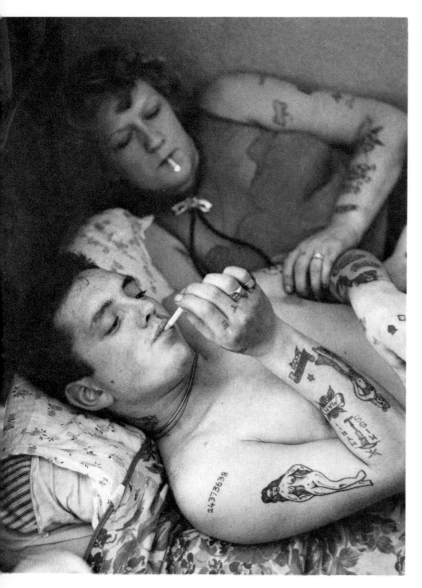

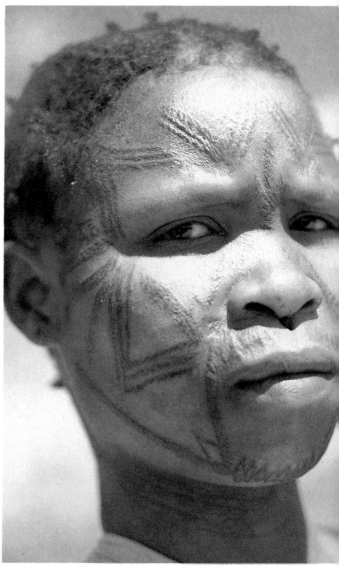

Tattooing (above left) can enhance the parts you never thought of. Lips, gums, genitals, the tip of the tongue, the stomach – none are safe from the needle. Originally designed to take the place of clothes as decoration in peoples who needed no clothes due to the climate or whose jobs rendered clothes, at any rate on the top half, superfluous (the Navy, coal miners), tattooing has moved with the age of technology into a secret, cult thing. You only get to see it in intimacy. Unlike body painting which is closer to modern make-up, tattooing signals an irrevocable commitment. Nevertheless, Society, hell-bent on survival, generally adapted tattooing by the much more feasible means of decorated clothing rather than intentional permanent mutilation. The chilly West and North, where clothing was part of the survival kit, however chic it became, never adopted another irremediable beauty aid, body scoring (above right). However, the appeal of skin which is not too smooth, bland and familiar lingers on in Western man, especially since the introduction of central heating to the masses. Proof is provided by the fact that one of the most famous fur and leather goods designers in the world, Fendi of Rome, produced in 1978 a range of handbags and luggage in a fine glacé hide impressed with tribal scorings. Smart women everywhere, and smart men too, could be seen fingering this imitation of human Braille.

very public places (a railway carriage and a grand ball) whether they might stroke – they used the word 'touch', but 'caress' is what they meant – the fabric of what I was wearing. One instance was velvet, the other fur. Now these may seem very obvious turn-ons for private events but what made the experiences interesting to me was that both examples of their genre happened to be not just superb examples of their material in quality but both were unusually and very excitingly coloured. The velvet, a huge Henry VIII mantle, was patterned to resemble the complete plumage of a cock pheasant. The fur – baby foxes shaded pale to slate grey-blue – looked as soft as the marabou jackets onto which leisured ladies who need to spend the morning in bed for whatever reason spill Cooper's English Coarse Cut marmalade.

The long-to-touch-you catalogue of fabrics is interesting, for it ranges from the apparently implacable gabardines and worsted twills – which say, particularly in sporting dress, 'keep your hands off' but leave the impression of a lot of fun to be had under that dour and proper exterior – right through to the most innocent or calculated cheesecloth and chiffon.

The Empress Elisabeth of Austria certainly knew how to use fabric to the maximum sexual advantage, and to use colour, too. Habited in black menswear twill for the hunting field by Charles Creed, the British tailors, she was sewn into her jacket because no fastenings save seams were adequate for the discomfort she was prepared to face in order to cut a socially acceptable fashion figure at the same time as participating in a man's sport. The price to pay for riding better than half the men in the field (even if 'Bay' Middleton, her pilot, did grumble that she was too slow across the big fences) was a small one. Here was a woman, clothed and coloured as convention demanded, mastering a great horse. Heavens, what must she be like in bed?

And then, at night, a misty vision of spangled pale tulle, innocence and propriety – and yet all these posed questions for the hopeful admirer.

In talking of colour as an erotic stimulus both white and black are already well documented. Black is the classic concept of domination – the evil man, the baddy, the executioner – or it is the garb of chastity, bureaucracy, sorrow, humble-pie eaters. I have often wondered whether the adjective 'creepy' does not derive from the fabric crêpe, so beloved of the sorrowful. The point about black is that it is the single most flattering of all colours to wear, enhancing the dingiest skin and any colour of hair. White takes more getting away with, and has complex social overtones of purity, ice-coldness, virginity, youth and general inexperience of sex, which is why it was adopted in the

133

West as a suitable colour for brides after the invention of the wedding dress in the twentieth century. You must remember that until World War II or maybe just before, people were married in their very, very best frock, which was then cut about to make into an evening ensemble of some sort, but was in the height of whatever fashion was going on. After World War II wedding dresses are the first real fancy dresses, and though they do tend in the Establishment bracket to be white, this could be seen as Society's joke against Authority yet again because as the chances of the bride being a virgin, entitled to the vestal colour, get slimmer, so it seems the determination of Society grows to scoot around the problem by appearing in fancy dress at the alter.

Only two other colours really count in terms of eroticism. Scarlet. The scarlet woman. Don Giovanni always wore scarlet, so do the better-dressed devils. Scarlet says, 'Look at me, and want me.' Scarlet is for the conspicuous.

Navy blue is for the quietly dangerous. No clever woman should ever disregard the prim allure of this halfway house between black and white. One of the world's least flattering of shades, navy blue has implications of security, modesty, touch-me-not that can be a powerful influence, particularly on a weak man, not quite sure of himself.

Both red and purple have an indirect sexual allure in that they are colours associated with temporal or spiritual power. Purple is the only actual colour (as opposed to tissue) ever reserved for the highest and unavailable to lesser ranks; the reasoning behind it, as with the reservation of silk to certain personages, was not that one was liable to look such a wow in it that everyone else would be knocked out of the competition, but the hard-nosed economic one that purple was an extraordinarily difficult and expensive dye to produce and obtain.

Hovering between the appeal of fabric and the lure of colour must come beaded clothes. If Dorothy Parker slid into satin, the poet W.B. Yeats would have been charmed by Schiaparelli, Hartnell, or the American, Norman Norell: 'Had I the heaven's embroidered cloths, Enwrought with golden and silver light, The blue, and the dim, and the dark cloths Of night and light and the half-light . . .' Yeats could be echoing teenagers' dreams of what they would like to wear to the disco. Or, even more, what they want to see their stage idols in. I am not aware that anyone has measured the precise sexual effect of stage clothes allied to raw music, or whether it is possible to compute the balance of decibel screams from the audience in relation not just to the decibels blasted from the stage but to the degree of shine of one sort or another on the performer's torso. The satin and beads stop and the glistening, sweating flesh begins, shiny too. I should think someone could do a PhD thesis on orgasms per spangle.

And then there is the sound of materials. Swish. Rustle. Whisper. Starchy crackle. Rip.

For a great many men it is the smell of materials which is exciting. Once again, the range of tastes is inexhaustible. A court case which hit the British headlines in 1980 revolved around a postal traffic in dirty knickers. At the polar opposite must come the crisp, freshly ironed smell of nursery laundry, of idyllic country mornings, of clothes fresh from the wind-blown line. Somewhere between total innocence, and nostalgia for the days before responsibility bowed the shoulders and fading virility induced a quirk, come all the choice of animal smells of fur and leather, animal smells doused by exotic overtones of flowers. Long after the lover is gone, the memory of the scent of the clothes, be it of armpits or Arpège, lingers on. There is also a great satisfaction in knowing the smell of one's own clothes. After all, if the outcome of that particular encounter was not what you had hoped for, you can always pop it into the coin-op and start all over again. Fashion writers are always telling their readers never to apply scent directly onto their clothes on the grounds that it will either burn a hole in them or go stale. I have never advocated this theory. Many scents do stain, some do go stale, but on balance it's worth the gamble.

7 LET RIP

Why are the nicest presents always gift-wrapped? Why do shops spend a fortune on decorating their parcels with quite unnecessary bows and loops of ribbon? Why is it that brown-paper parcels are more exciting in direct ratio to the number of unassailable knots? In order to double the anticipation, to force the eager hands to fight for what they hope to possess, to cut through knots and rip aside bows until at last the secret trinket is revealed. To many people that fact that the contents of the package may be a saucepan or a diamond necklace seems to matter much less than the tremendous fun and stimulation of undoing things.

Similarly, the most obviously exciting adjuncts to clothing are the fastenings. As with a present, appearance is all, and the more deliciously superfluous the bows, the more obdurate the knotted belts, the more and the longer the zip fasteners, the better the contents are going to seem when they are finally handed over.

There is a wealth of religious symbolism in fastening knots and bows; the woollen girdle of Greek brides was woven in a snaky design similar to the decoration chosen by Mercury for his wand in the gift-wrapping department on Olympus, and was the symbol of their virginity. Their husband was now going to have the fun of untying the parcel. It is tempting to conjecture whether the plainer brides tied more complex knots to work up a bit of excitement before their defloration – which is what untying is all about. It was one of the labours of Hercules to steal the girdle of Hippolyta, the Amazon (therefore virgin) queen, i.e. to get her into bed. The goddess of love and beauty, Venus, even had a name for her girdle. It was called Cestus, and was made for her by her husband, Vulcan, the

Apollo, god of music and the arts, obviously took time off for other pursuits. Armed with his laurel tree regalia, placed at a somewhat ambivalent angle one might think, he chases one of the Muses for inspiration. What he grasps first is of course her girdle, which signifies her virginity. In this case there is the much more subtle point that if he can 'rape', or gain access to, one of the Muses, whom the *Oxford Classical Dictionary* describes as 'among the most lovable and most influential creations; personification of the highest intellectual and artistic aspirations', his creative power is assured.

blacksmith of the gods. Unfortunately when Mars, god of war, who presumably needed a good deal of running repairs to his weaponry, was coming round to the Vulcan household for fittings and the old boy was bashing about in the forge, he took a great fancy to Mrs V. and her girdle fell off. Since her husband was a blacksmith, one can assume that it was a particularly obdurate type of girdle to remove, and may indeed be the earliest record of a metal chastity belt. It was last sighted on the 'Acidalian Mount' and is credited with the power to move to ardent love. Exceptionally sexy women are still described poetically as wearing Aphrodite's girdle (Aphrodite being the Greek equivalent of Venus) just as in poetic terms the female pudenda is called Venus' mount.

There have been cads about from the dawn of time so it should be recorded that Alexander the Great set an interesting precedent when confronted with the Gordian knot, worthy of the Post Office and popularly thought to be un-doable. He just cut straight through it with his sword, no messing about. Mind you, he knew what was in the parcel – the kingship of the whole East – but then most determined rakes who do not mess about know what they are after, even if they are but temporary kings.

The direct sexual link with untying persisted in rural communities until the last hundred years, when it was customary for a young man

Parlez-vous Franglais? The French word for a riding coat was 'redingote', and by 1800 French women had got their hands onto this practical item of menswear and made it a high fashion item. It had capes and stout fastenings to resist a long clop over muddy roads, but Madame transformed it by using fine broadcloth embellished with delicious satin fastenings designed to look like lacings and ending in a bow below the breasts.

137

to give the object of his attentions a pair of laced shoes. If she accepted them, she accepted him, with the implicit understanding that he would be allowed to untie them and take them off, in other words to have her virginity.

There is a theory that you can tell everything about designers' attitudes to women by the way they tie their bows. I would take the principle further and say that you can tell everything about designers' attitudes to women by the way they fasten their dresses. Jean Muir, for example. Such a calm, subfusc perfection, such an exquisite attention to neat and orderly dress. A little prim, a little dour even, some think. But then look at the buttons, rows and rows of tiny covered buttons, calling out for help to do up and exciting in the extreme in the prospect of the undoing. I have always thought that Jean Muir's clothes are not for women of immediate and abundant physical attraction, they are for women who lodge in a man's mind, tremendously sophisticated, cool and choosy. They are the fastenings for the clothes of a woman who has to play a more subtle game. They are not for cloddish lovers, who would probably rip the silk crêpe de chine button-loops.

French haute couture with its rigid tradition has always put bows on the dresses which used to be described as 'jeune fille'. Hideous as they were, they did make a statement in a Catholic country about the status of the wearer. She was a young virgin, and if the bow had been put on the dress by Dior, then she was a young, rich virgin, too: so much the better, went the signalling system. Play it right, and you too could untie that girdle and live in the Avenue Montaigne or somewhere equally salubrious. The French themselves pretty quickly realised that in 1960 jeunes filles and virginity and marrying the right duc did not necessarily go together, and the bows on the party dresses got stuck where they belonged, in minor houses with a stuffy clientèle.

However, the designers had reckoned without the Americans; or more accurately, the creative ones had reckoned without the Americans, but their business managers had not. America is the land of the young still, with almost impossibly demanding physical, in other words virility, symbols expected from even its most distinguished older personalities. To be 'old' is to be on the sexual scrapheap, so everybody who can gets a remould. The pain, the time, the expense, the mind-time now used up in America in meddling with what God gave us rivals the sophistication of the Far East and the ingenuity of the primitive tribes.

To a wide section of American society the bow is the symbol of girlishness. No sooner have the over-fifties had the wrinkles ironed out and their bottoms hoisted back into tennis-dress shape than they

Madame de Pompadour had dear little bows all down her front, Queen Alexandra had the same thing in diamonds and in 1964 André Courrèges, the reigning star then of French couture, produced this invitation to the undoing of womanhood. With a twitch you unlock her face for a kiss and, moving at the pace you choose, you may then untie her bosom and eventually her loins. These fastenings are at the polar extreme from the sturdy and practical lacings of the honest peasant, presenting as they do a woman as a box of chocolates, gift-wrapped. Before unwrapping, be sure that the centres are going to be to your taste.

are hard at it putting bows in their hair. The bows go with the dress of a culture in which the females describe themselves as 'girls' at the age of sixty and under the influence of many blue rinses, and with the dress of a society (parallelled in many other countries) in which high-powered women and very masculine women quite unconsciously believe that a pussy-cat bow on the blouse under their tweed suit makes them look ultra-feminine. Known as the softening touch, all it is is sickeningly hypocritical to fashion purists.

Anyway, the Americans being such very important customers of the French couture, after World War II the designers, who had at first held them at bay with wildly uncomfortable and very mature chic, found the new wealth getting frisky, as it always does eventually, and demanding youthful splendour. The French immediately thought up bows, a feature after all deeply ingrained in their cultural and religious background. We were therefore confronted for a decade with bows. There were bows spiteful, bows resigned, bows to make fools of the women who wore them. Cestus reigned again, although whether her presence evoked quite such hoped-for results is arguable.

There are two designers who can tie a cunning knot, and for the same reason. They are Zandra Rhodes – who swathes the waists of silk tulle crinolines with satin ties which would look well around a coffret of chocolates from Charbonnel and Walker or a diamond from

139

Fastenings for fastening's sake. President Kennedy's mother used to complain that it took herself and the nursemaids half an hour to get her substantial brood buttoned into their warm winter gaiters. The interesting point of this picture is that, as with children's gaiters or back-laced corsets, the construction of the garment pre-supposes the presence of another party in the putting on of the attire, who is presumably also on hand to take it off.

Harry Winston – and Valentino. They succeed because both love the beauty of women and see it at its most attractive as innocent and unspoiled. For these two designers, the bow fastening is not just a deliberate trim on a refrigerator, or a refrigerated woman, it is a loving and submissive gesture to those who understand and admire the wearing or the viewing of an ancient, ever-powerful symbol.

Lacings can best be set under practicality; a comforting and simple method to gather up the aching muscles and support for the work-worn torso, and a practical garb for women who needed to pop out a breast to an infant. Then they should be set under fashion, and eventually fetishism. In the eighteenth century lacings over an underbodice vied with delectable bows in suggesting the earthy appeal of peasant dress. When lacing went under cover or initially round the back, which of course meant that it was about to become a cult, not a practicality, the first to complain was Rabelais (1495–1553) because, with lacing up the back, he was no longer able to unlatch a couple of notches, rather in the way we loosen our tennis shoes, and fondle a breast, just as we scratch our instep.

Moved from outerwear to innerwear, lacing became the most obvious adjunct of the corset, which has been fully discussed in the previous chapter.

Zips have had a slow rise to general acceptability as a sex symbol, possibly because they are just too overtly aggressive and sexually threatening. When they were first introduced by Schiaparelli in the 'thirties, Authority applauded in the name of scientific advance (the Church kept mum; they were not going to give up all those adorable little buttons) and Society felt it right that their privileges in the shape of made-to-measure high-style clothes might be brought a touch closer to the common masses (who were getting a bit restive and might be needed to fight Hitler) by this clever and ingenious little whim of darling Elsa's – so inexpensive, mes chères.

The zip, however, very quickly proved that it needed propping from neither scientific greybeards nor democratic smarties to survive. It was immediately apparent to those who read between the lines that it was superbly erotic. That swift, sure closure – now you see it, now you don't – that slow descent, with at any moment the brakes full on. It was like getting up and down the Alps on a cable-car, negotiating all those tiny teeth. Yes, teeth. Move too fast, be clumsy, and you get bitten – just a blood blister perhaps, but a passion mark none the less.

Now, you did not get bitten by buttons or bows and so it is perhaps the element of physical danger, the chance of flesh being mauled by steel, which gives zips their special erotic appeal. That that appeal is widely disseminated is proved by the fact that it is a major source of

140

excitement to the extreme fetishist macho group, to a limbo of respectable housewives, to an entirely novel 1970s phenomenon called Punk dressing, and ever and anon to the hautest of haute couture.

Any opening and closing which looks simple to operate incites the enjoyment of the peep-show. Stolid historians of the fourteenth and fifteenth centuries tend to allocate the fashion for 'slashed' dress (and slashed shoes) to necessity: ragged trousers in need of patching and aching feet in need of slippered comfort. Maybe, for about five minutes. The historians are wrong on both counts. Slashed dress is the precursor of black leather trousers with fourteen zips in them, none there for any reason save expectancy, not expediency.

In the middle ground, housewives tend to prefer zippered boots, which poses the question of whether they are unprepared to make the sacrifice demanded by pulling on and pulling off, as well as actually squelching around in, very tight-fitting leg and footwear, or whether the zipper affords to some a practical comfort which is in itself quite a pleasing ritual – sinking down on the favourite chair, work all done, animals and family fed, and now to unzip the friendly footwear. Good as a cup of tea. Unconsciously, some may like the dominant suggestion implicit in heavy-duty zipping. Rulers of the world wore boots, didn't they, and you have to say that Sharon looks neat up there behind Dave on the Honda. My, that bike is as big as a horse. Must take a lot of mastering.

Punk was the 1979 equivalent of the slashing of the Renaissance age, and one could draw some interesting analogies as to its initiation and popularity. In 1477 the Swiss won a battle against the Duke of Burgundy and, tattered in the extreme, patched up their clothes with the textile spoils of war. Since they were the victors, and everyone likes the winner, their costume was quickly aped, to the extent that Michelangelo, in designing the outfits for the Swiss papal guard, popped them into slashed doublets which lasted long enough to

Above left: Easy on, easy off? Motor-bike messenger boys in a French café, one of them sporting no less than eight zips on his jacket. You too could get a special delivery.

Above right: Girls as luggage, something you cart about with you and lose at airports perhaps. This lovely piece of baggage is as simple to unfasten and enter as your Louis Vuiton or Mark Cross suitcase.

141

Not the moment for fumbling fingers – or is it? Apparently the easy prey, these ladies (above left) can afford to be choosy.

Peep show (above right). Slashed garments originated when a tattered but victorious army struggled home and was duly lauded. Fashion quickly noted the possibilities of double-decker dress. This fine figure of a man of the mid-sixteenth century is positively covered with the cuts which might have been expected in serious swordplay but which, turned into high style, suggest delights beneath. Note the unmatched stockings: they could give heart to mothers of schoolchildren groping around in dawn's early light for a matched pair, though it is possible that the headmaster will not view the arrangement as at all erotic.

witness the attempt on the life of John Paul II in 1981. Having been the design of need, the many-apertured garment thus became the mark of fashionable power.

The upholders of the Punk dynasty were not fighting the Duke of Burgundy; they were fighting Authority in the guise of the police and all the drabness and boredom and sterility of life for which they stood, and they were fighting the yobs, the skinheads, the bovver-booters and the crude vandals who seemed set to demolish everything that was visually or audibly attractive and enjoyable. Ragged armies are hard to maintain in a Welfare State, and so the sartorial protest, though undoubtedly patched together initially with scraps from market stalls and other sources of remarkably cheap fabrics and above all of remarkably cheap zips, was probably funded from student grants paid by the taxpayer. It took no time at all for the listening public to adopt, and punk became within months high fashion. In every drawing-room, chic and wealthy women were to be seen with holes in the most remarkable places on their apparel. They (the holes, I mean) were best outlined with hand-sewn seed pearls. Well, the glittery Elizabethans liked a pearl or two around their slashings. Thus is need adopted by leisure. Its stimulating connotations remain the same.

So we come to the zip in haute couture and for this I can provide no more apposite or amusing story than that told me by Hubert de Givenchy. De Givenchy dresses some of the most rich, beautiful and

142

above all determined women in the world. He does not set a 'line' but dresses the individual at her command and she is his inspiration. His is the most conspiratorial of couture. So, confronted with an order for a very special dress for a very specially intimate occasion by a very self-aware client, the comte did what any good designer would do in the circumstances: he enquired, with the utmost discretion, what Madame hoped would be the outcome of the evening, so that his dress would be both appropriate and equal to the occasion.

'Oh, that's quite simple,' she replied. 'I want it very high to the neck, with long, tight sleeves and a skirt to the floor. And a very, very long zip down the back.' That the zip will have been put in by hand, that it will in fact have been quite invisible in the couture masterpiece which he devised for her, only makes the whole thing even more erotic. She seemed to be seamless, this lovely creature, so elegant and assured, but where was the entry, the zip to Paradise? What fun the fondling must have been to find out how the damn' thing was got into. As exciting as running the fingers over the back of a woman from a tribe which needed no clothes and so with her sexual key incised on her back.

Having already reserved my right to be selective rather than definitive in what constitutes erotic dress, there are none the less gaps which it behoves me to fill, if only to explain why I have not written about them. Thus the manufacturers of hooks and eyes, of press-studs and of that novelty, Velcro, should not immediately cancel their subscription to a press-cutting agency for failing to find a reference to themselves in this book. To be blunt, press-studs and hooks and eyes have always struck me as quite extraordinarily unsexy and not aesthetically pleasing. After all those hours spent stitching them over in matching thread they are simply too practical. You cannot tighten them, as with laces, nor can you rip them as with a zip. Indeed, their most frequent use in modern dress is as a single item just above that naughty zip, or in pairs or in multiples on the sort of elastomeric figure-supporters favoured by women who require such things. In the prim 'fifties, it is true, there could have been a volume written on the proper technique for getting off padded brassières with these intractable fastenings (at the back) quickly enough to retain the moment of exultant expectancy and certainly before the débutante realised what you were up to, slapped your face, thought better of it, or went home to Mummy.

As for Velcro, well, that has indeed a sexy parentage since it was devised after a Swiss scientist had observed two burrs tumbling down a hill, locked in indissoluble embrace by their own little hooks given them by Nature. Since I am not an authority on the sexing of burrs, I cannot say whether their union was ecstatic, profligate,

Many clothes can be peeled off like a banana skin, but the spiral zip on this 1981 dress from Azzedine Alaïa of Paris enables the male to denude a woman like an orange.

143

productive or just that they happened to bump into one another on the mountainside and no sooner could they say 'What's the price of tomatoes at your supermarket' than they were away.

What I can say, though, is that if Velcro belongs anywhere in *Skin to Skin* I would have somehow to work it into the section on pain in the next chapter, since I understand from those who have tried fastening their trousers or their shower-curtains with it that they experience agony when trying to effect a quick exit from inside either because their body hairs are mistaken by the dutiful closure for its mate. Nylon may feel no pain when ripped apart. Flesh does.

8 PERILOUS PLEASURES

To my knowledge, nobody has recorded the feelings of all those hapless maidens chained up in mythology to various bits of the landscape wearing scanty if any clothing when the hero eventually arrived to rescue them, but my bet is that they were mixed. Frequently, his mode of travel was novel, if not unprecedented, and the first thing that he did, without so much as a 'good afternoon', was to dismember their guard monster of which, after several aeons, they had become rather fond. True, its conversation and cooking were limited – one can tire oh so quickly of charred titbits of failed rescuers – but having it snuffling around was quite cosy, and it had the dearest little wings and whiskers, and after all it never hurt them, it merely flame-gunned intruders.

But has anybody ever suggested that Andromeda took one look at Perseus and told him straight out that he was a boorish arriviste with a nasty carnal glint in his eye and a very alarming huge lance which he was preparing to poke into the open mouth of her personal dragon; and so that all in all, if he would just care to drop in next time he was passing with some light reading and a couple of new negligées, she would be grateful if he would stop parking that weird flying machine on her patch.

For his part, it is taken as read that Perseus found the lady irresistible. There is no mention of an inclination to dump her when he discovered that she was a trifle older than he had been led to expect, or a bit weather-beaten after all that exposure, or just simply not his type.

Nor should anti-vivisectionists and members of the RSPCA lose sleep over the fate of the dragon. He put up a terrific fight, the whole

145

Bondage at its most enchanting is innocent beauty not only in distress but above all tied up and protected by a fearsome beast which could be interpreted as anyone's mother-in-law. Perseus arrives on a distinctly zappy type of horse/bird to rescue the wilting Andromeda. Feminists should side with the beast, the romantically inclined with handsome Perseus, while anyone unable to make up their mind could opt for the horse/bird, who is aesthetically very pleasing.

party was very exciting and glamorous (after all he had said 'no way' to lots of dreary men who simply did not have the equipment, the technique or the dress to command the situation), and so his dying pangs were possibly exquisite at the hands of this super-male.

The fact that in this particular instance of bondage, rescue and rape Andromeda's plight was occasioned by her boastful and over-protective mother has probably given rise to the interpretation of this type of myth by both Jung and Freud as the freeing of the anima by some outer force (Perseus) from the devouring (poor old dragon) aspect of the mother. But this is to assume that the monster threatens

146

the girl, and must be killed. A more lively and likely interpretation is that the monster threatens the man, for he is symbolic of the woman's maidenhood; he is the 'toothed vagina', the vagina hedged around with moral principles, religious considerations, physical distaste or fright – as dangerous and as hard to surmount as any fortification or a besieged city, yet barring the way to untold delights.

In order to spur on the champion, whose energy problem by now might have induced him to go home to a TV dinner and to forget trying to stick his lance into a mouth so full of danger, the lady is tied up; to make him feel more the man, to arouse him, she is hapless, beseeching. In other words, Andromeda could have looked like a sack of potatoes for all Perseus would have cared by the time he had hoisted in all those chains and dragons, amid whimpering and general hassle. It could be a fun occasion, and just what should he wear?

'One deviant sexual fantasy so frequently and urgently expressed in European art . . . concerns the plight of the bound and helpless victim,' writes Edward Lucie-Smith in *Eroticism in Western Art*. It is also expressed in Western dress, perhaps more so now than at any previous date, or perhaps it is just that Society is more frank about its sado-masochistic tastes in clothing and that the media are more prepared to advise the world on the subject. Many collections of clothes by established designers contain blatant suggestion of sado-masochistic inclinations; the whole punk dress movement of the 1980s was fashion's flip-side reaction to a movement which had been

St Agatha was tortured and murdered at Catania in Sicily, probably around 250 AD. Sebastiano del Piombo painted her as he imagined her ordeal began. The picture illustrates the artist's freedom to show with impunity the most sadistic and therefore possibly erotic scenes under the guise of religious art; sadism has often found a stronghold in the Church.

gaining momentum over the past ten years. Fashion always has a laugh up its sleeve if it is to remain important with hindsight and not just to be dismissed as a freak cult for initiates only. Thus while it would be quite wrong to suggest that, with punk, SM dressing reached the status and the respectability of mass-market acceptance, nevertheless having a lot of young people hopping up and down our city streets with their knees chained together with dog-leashes does mean that an age-old human fantasy of clothing is alive and well and being worn to the disco in Bermondsey or Brooklyn.

Interestingly enough, precisely the level of watered-down sexual aggression was occasioned as their watered-down version of the ultimate SM gear invited. On the whole, the punks tended to be limp-wristed, submissive, unable to flee because of all those chains on their arms, legs, noses and ears, and covered in such very suggestive holes in their clothing as to invite the lance, literal or metaphorical. Thus it should come as no wonder that they were chased, beaten up, seduced, rescued and conquered or a bit of all by Perseus figures from rival gangs, equally distinctive in their dress, who were excited to acts of great cruelty by these surrogate bondees.

There is a medical term, algolagnia (algos, pain; lagnia, voluptuousness) which describes a condition in which physical pain or distress or fear either by a participant or by a voyeur stimulates sexual pleasure to a profound degree. Having nothing whatever of the martyr in my own make-up, I was relieved to find that Mr Lucie-Smith also finds the expression on the faces of female saints being put to death in overtly sexual manners as somewhat ambivalent.

Since this is not a book about the psychology of sexual quirks, but of the dress which accompanies them in their most bland or most profligate manifestation, I ask readers to allow me to be simplistic in suggesting the two major causes of Society seeking release via somewhat unusual methods of behaviour and clothing could be summarised under the headings of boredom and guilt. Boredom, since it is usually the product of leisure although it may now be within the grasp of the unoccupied but State-funded person of low intelligence, has through history been a peril to more sophisticated and investigative minds. Thus the classic chronicle of such practices was written by a French aristocrat of the eighteenth century, the Marquis de Sade. With plenty of peasants, definitely not State-supported, to do everything for him, the voluptuary was free from scratching a living to enjoy his enjoyment of pain as a sexual stimulant.

It is in this particular aspect of dress for sexually deviant practices that fashion brushes her skirts against crime. The most popular outfits for the 'executioner' rôle are based upon the traditional gear of

The stage where it stops being funny and starts getting dangerous. Potentially suffocating dress from Atomage of London.

148

the professional killer – black, brawny, inhuman in response to pleas for mercy because masked and therefore depersonalised. Note the similarities between modern terrorist gangs, in their balaclavas or with stockings over their faces, the ritual dress of the Ku Klux Klan, and the sort of figure you might expect to see hovering above you if you were unlucky enough to come round between the hanging and the disembowelling chapters of your death.

For the Jack Ketchs of history this dress, now so terrifying and sinister, was both practical and ergonomic. First, it helped to be hooded. After all, you had no personal grudge against the wretched victim, it was all part of your job, and you were cool enough to kneel and ask his forgiveness for what you were about to have to do and not above accepting a tip to do it well. This implied no restriction of movement from the shape or cut of your clothing as you wielded the instruments of death and also great durability of material; hence the popularity of leather which, in those days of primitive tanning, would have been hard and impossible to join together except by metal studs.

A point worth noting: a study of the dress of executioners suggests that it is only since a minor glow of civilisation, or guilty conscience at the horrors about to be performed, has struck Western man that such formal disguise has been deemed appropriate. In antique plates, and indeed in pictures of modern executions in less developed areas of the world, the executioner is indistinguishable from his victim in social connotations of dress.

As for guilt, the bank manager, let us say, prop and stay of his community, yet interiorly suppressed, is a likely customer for Atomage, a shop which specialises in just such black-leather, studded, menacing gear. By day, he must wear a neat suit and tell you yes, you can have an overdraft. But in his private life he can enact all the fantasies of the gauleiter which he would dearly like to perpetrate on his tiresome, whining customers. I have no statistics on the escape-routes chosen by persons in service industries, emasculated by the whims of their necessary clients ('No, of course that steak is quite wrong, sir.' Thinks – he comes here twice a week and never spends less than £90) but if I had to take an inspired guess I would decide that while restaurateurs go on the bottle, and artists and designers onto cocaine, many mice among men whisk home and change into dominant dress. Designers and artists can wear what they like, as can restaurateurs, so other options slot into their life by way of addiction; the formalised man seeks release in dress furthest away from what he is forced to wear. He becomes a sexual force again, workaday or matrimonial emasculation forgotten.

The dress of the 'executioner' is one criminal aspect of bondage

If you thought that wives waiting behind the door with a rolling pin to berate their drunken or otherwise errant husbands upon their return was a music-hall joke not older than the nineteenth century, think again. Women have been wearing the breeches, by virtue of their breasts, for thousands of years. Martin Treu, an artist of the sixteenth century in Germany, well illustrated the dilemma of pain and pleasure.

149

dressing for erotic stimulus. The other aspect is far more dangerous because the clothes involved in this sort of sex play can cause death. In 1981 a British policeman was tried for the murder of a lesbian prostitute. He had attached her, as a 'punishment' for being late (she was late deliberately, it seems, thereby inviting the scenario that she knew would follow) to a wooden cross on the wall. She was muffled in typical bondage clothes, and she suffocated.

After all this heavy-breathing stuff it is pleasant to be able to report at least two instances in which fashion has insisted on displaying its natural wit and irreverence. A woman interviewed by Gosselin and Wilson in their book, *Sexual Variations*, let slip the information that during a sado-masochistic game with her husband, which they regularly played, he had tied her down ready to receive 'punishment'. Presumably she had been stripped while he was wearing heavy boots, for 'as he walked by he kicked my heel with his toe by mistake. I gave a yelp, and he said, "Sorry love, did I hurt you?"' In 1910 a French pharmacist, Jean Parat, was arrested when police found his wife chained to the bed wearing under her clothes a chain-mail corset padlocked around her waist. Brought to trial, Parat defended his behaviour by pointing out that the chains were designed to be long enough to allow her to play the piano. The piano? What on earth do you suppose the good lady chose for her repertoire? *Fidelio*? There are some manacles around in that.

Both transvestitism and fetishism are basically selfish forms of deviation, and neither is very interesting in fashion terms. For the purposes of this book they have provided nothing very subtle in the way of clothing, deriving in both instances as sexual turn-ons from an existing erogenous pattern rather than producing some strange retrospective or imaginative canto in the history of fashion. Yes, transvestites wear the dress of women or vice versa, because they wish to be free to express the dual nature of the sex of most thinking people within a society no longer terrified by the need for procreation into a sharp division of progenitors. Yes, fetishists quite frequently pick an object of apparel as an object of adoration, but it is likely to be a pair of shoes picked up on any major thoroughfare, or a textile which has in their mind some special sexy properties.

One area of transvestite dressing which one should examine, though, is its transformation from a dress of punishment to a dress of pleasure. Nineteenth-century literature in particular is filled with torrid quasi-fictional, quasi-autobiographical accounts of boys being dressed as girls as a penance for some real or imagined misdemeanour. Now, for centuries small children of either sex had been dressed alike – in skirts. The reasons provided for this range among fashion commentators from the assumptions of practicality – large families

Lock up your daughters. Haute couture's joke at the expense of fetishism was to produce very expensive metal 'dresses' and headgear. Worn over an impregnable lurex body-stocking, itself worn over some doughty underpinnings, the out-fit looks as improbable as that devised by Hollywood for Cleopatra (page 117).

150

could just swop clothes until necessity in the shape of ergonomics of work and movement made unisex dress, at any rate in the female mould, useless – to the superstitious, which held that since the spite of the gods was directed at the magic male, he should be disguised as a female until old enough to fend for himself.

Authority has always imposed either special dress, or special lack of dress, on its victims (in the reign of Edward II, 'condemned for high treason, Thomas, earl of Lancaster, was first diposed of his armour and then clothed in a robe of raye that had belonged to his esquire'), including the designation of the colour yellow as that for fools, penitents or Jews. It got its due come-uppance as usual at the hands of individuals. A woman condemned to wear the letter 'A' on her breast by the puritans of New England because she had committed adultery in the mid-seventeenth century is noted by a later historian as having 'sported with her infamy'. The 'lost and desperate creature' embroidered the 'fatal token' in scarlet cloth with golden thread and the 'nicest art of needlework; so that the capital A might have been thought to mean Admirable, or anything rather than Adulteress'.

But in Society at large, the imposition of female dress upon the male as a punishment is both recent and short-lived. No one who moves in the world of designers could now be surprised if, just as a girl turns up one day in a Zandra Rhodes ball gown and the next day

Above left: By 1980 transvestitism caused few raised eyebrows, although at one particular fashion show by Vivienne Westwood, held in the eminently respectable Pillared Hall at Olympia in London, some older journalists were seen to blink when ravishing blonde models removed their smart coats – to show that they were fellas. This picture is from an amazing event staged by one of England's most outrageous talents, Andrew Logan. It is called the Alternative Miss World Competition.

Above right: The Hermaphrodite was nothing out of the ordinary in ancient Greece. Compounded of the two gods, Hermes and Aphrodite, who symbolised fertility and 'love' of the male and female gender, there are many statues and paintings of these ambivalent characters. It is anyone's guess whether this figure is – or was originally – a man or a woman.

151

LES BATTEUSES
D'HOMMES

PAR

SACHER-MASOCH

R. Dorn, Éditeur, 51, Rue Monsieur le Prince, Paris.

Ow! And she has a long whacking cane, too. To our more blasé eyes this Victorian example of a soft-porn photo (above left) is as funny as those blue movies on tap in your hotel bedroom because both are equally unconvincing. Getting this pair to pose in such wicked abandon in 1865 might have taken the same effort as it would have done, say, to get Doris Day to appear topless in our own time.

Whipping and being whipped is described as 'le vice Anglais' because the over-indulgence in this pastime at British public schools gave all too many Englishmen a penchant for painful pleasure. In 1906 it was all going on in Paris, too, though possibly, given the French instinct for attracting the tourist trade and their underlying hatred of the English, it may have been foreigners who were destined to feel the birch of this delicious lady (above right). Clothes for sport have changed little in a century.

in slacks and a T-shirt, men now may appear, if not in the Ritz hotel (though their make-up and hair is so exquisite it might baffle dimmer maîtres d'hôtel), certainly in your house or your office one day in a vested suit, next in a mini, mauve wig and fish-net tights.

Thus the whisk from degradation to delight within the space of a hundred years. For the detached observer it is worth noting that cases of exceptional sartorial cruelty usually occur when women are themselves greatly repressed. Henry Spencer Ashbee, Pisanus Fraxi or Pornographer Royal, as you prefer to view him, wrote in 1877: 'Women delight in administering the birch; and innumerable are the tales of schoolmistresses whipping their pupils, mothers and especially mothers-in-law their children, and taking grim pleasure in the operation. Indeed women are more cruel and relentless than men.' Well we all know that, but what I long to know is whether they wore gloves as do modern wielders of the whip, so I am credibly informed. The other point which seems very unsatisfactorily resolved, at any rate by Ashbee, is where were all the men when this whipping was going on? A great number of the highest and humblest were being beaten black by schoolmasters it is true, but this seems to suggest that flagellation, 'the English Vice', mostly took place between persons of at any rate outwardly the same sex. So was the dressing of boys as girls as a penance merely an opportunity to extend their range of delicious bloodied buttocks by the terrifying females of the period?

152

9 FUTURE IMPERFECT

I BEGAN this book with the premise that any dress or bodily decoration – paraphernalia – above and beyond that necessary for survival has as its inspiration the desire to gratify the wearer or to inflame the interest of somebody else. Viewed as an incitement to brave all in the sexual lists, dress has shown itself to be the best weapon with which to arm for a game without limits, a jeu sans frontières. What else can gratify the longing for heroes, or the fantasy of being someone else for a few hours? Dress can seduce by touch, by smell, by colour, by size (big or little, take your choice), it invokes sentimental or frightful memories, it provokes aggression and also soothes the nervous, who feel better with an Establishment label stitched on somewhere. It can symbolise power, it unwraps to lace-frothed submission. In fact, dress is the game at which anyone can be good, which is more than you can say for cricket or baseball.

If the principles upon which stimulating dressing are based remain the same, what will keep changing is the living context in which the dress is worn. It is for this reason that designers and fashion commentators with sense and sensibility are so reluctant to commit themselves to prognostications. The former know that they are but the sartorial transmission stations for a human desire to be more alluring, and the latter mostly come to a full stop with the arrival in Paris of blue jeans.

Designers have had a singular failure in dressing numerous film and TV interpretations of what we will be wearing to look chic disembarking from the shuttle plane not just to Glasgow or Boston but to Mars. These have ranged from, in the charitable view, unconvincing, to the Prudence Glynn view that they are ludicrous. Who

153

One designer's idea of what the future holds in store. This cuirasse by Paco Rabanne is in body-forming shiny plastic. It is heavily laced, combines brassière with tease – is she really that shape underneath? – and is fastened with just two pretty bows. It is comparable, perhaps, to the nippled armour of the neo-classical period, although obviously men did not need front fastenings.

could imagine a good old-fashioned sex-orgy aboard Battlestar Galactica? Though I suppose that long, neon-lit prods of incalculable power, while looking to me like the lighting from a late-night take-away in a poor section of town, may have phallic symbolism for some. I am unable to look forward to a close encounter with Batman and intend to plead a headache, which he, silly softy, will be taken in by. Questioned, viewers of a series called 'Buck Rogers in the 25th Century' state that the only alluring figure in the plot is dressed in black-leather motor-cycling gear and is wearing a bird's head mask.

The fashion commentators' most illustrious perpetrator of the howler ought to be John Carl Flügel. In his book, *The Psychology of Clothes*, he remarks, amidst a closet full of what I believe to be misinterpretations about the role of dress: 'We must honestly face the conclusion that our principle points ultimately not to clothing but to nakedness . . . Dress is after all destined to be but an episode in the history of humanity and man (and perhaps before him, woman) will one day go about his business secure in the control of his body and of his wider physical environment, disdaining the sartorial crutches on which he perilously supported himself during the earlier tottering stages of his march towards a higher culture.'

While he is quite right in saying that 'fashion' is an episode in the history of mankind (and a twentieth-century phenomenon, as I have argued elsewhere), dress is of another stuff. Dress is the stuff of dreams and of a continuing species.

Why are all the clothes in predictions of the future so dreary? Because they are sterile. They are not designed to persuade men and women to continue to fight for procreation. They are not erotic.

Flügel is apparently looking forward to a Wimbledon-in-the-skies final played between woad-painted successors of Bjorn Borg, perhaps with diamonds in their teeth, otherwise naked. What he has not taken into account is that the All-England Club, regarded now as a restrictionist joke, will be around in some form or another whenever or wherever; so will male vanity, authoritarian alarm and the allure of the covered.

Completely disagreeing with Flügel, I propose that man will wear more, not fewer, clothes in whatever future he has. The greater the leisure, the more perfect the climate, the greater the need for stimulation. The Greeks did it with conversation and leaps of the intellect, so perhaps in a world of artificial insemination and no nasty natural germs around we will go back to a simple plaid. I doubt it.

When all the universe is laid bare by science and technology man must retain mystery to unravel if he is not to expire from boredom. The bodies of the future may well be theoretically perfect, but then will they not be dreadfully alike – so uninspiring?

154

Unless something fearful has been done to the human mind in the interim, forced to look ahead I would suggest that the good old factors will apply. Faced even with perfection nobody is going to be content with it. With so much leisure and no need to worry about wrapping up against the cold, oh sex, rear thy lovely head. Let us live, and dress to live.

For now, you must excuse me. I have noticed, though not of course heard, the Rolls Royce at my door, and tonight is rather important. He will be clad in the contemporary robes of Savile Row, his acolytes similarly garbed, though they will have had to taxi to the restaurant since the Rolls is a part of his personal wardrobe, and he never allows people to borrow his clothes. That would be to threaten.

As for myself, well, I am after something, though with a strong idea in the back of my mind that the price we both have in view includes clauses unacceptable to either party. I have therefore 'dressed' with great care. What would Hubert de Givenchy have suggested confronted with this occasion, I wondered as I fondled from jeans to Yuki. Blond and tanned as I am from a long, hot summer, black with a slick cover-up of silver beads to match the London night-light seemed suitable.

If by now you have my next book on fashion resting – open, I trust, or at least with many pages with the corners turned down – on your coffee table then I am going to have proved Flügel wrong and the premise of *Skin to Skin* sound.

Above left: It looks like something out of science-fiction but is just something to wear down to the disco. While day clothes tend to be more and more prosaic and utilitarian, in the magic of after dark amazing transformations take place. Orange spiky hair with denims for 10 am to 6 pm, orange spiky hair plus a tuft or two, perhaps with gold lamé, Samurai garb, for 10 pm to 6 am.

The snake dresses of Cretan priestesses were imbued with magic power, and it was the original snake in Eden who started the whole sexual round-about. Polly Hope, the distinguished artist and designer, brings the jeu sans frontières to a constricting close with a dress made for a German client to wear at a smart party in 1980 (above right). It is not recorded how many were snared by the coils, but it does illustrate Society having the last word in the dress of power, privilege, fertility and intimacy, for who knows what the masterpiece might have cost?

155

INDEX

Adam 18–19, 23, 91, 105, 113, 151
Adam Ant 79
Addison, Joseph 71
Adrian, Gilbert 119
Agatha, Saint 147
Alaïa, Azzedine 143
Alexander the Great 137
Alexandra, Queen 55, 139
Alexandra, Princess 88
Amies, Hardy 58, 94
Amin, Idi 86
Andromeda 101, 117, 145–7
Aphrodite 137, 151, *see also* Venus
Apollo 137
armour 43, 59, 70, 71–3, 74, 83, 86, 154
arms 52–4, 62, 80, 81
Ashbee, Henry Spencer 152
Askew, Anne 82
Atomage 148, 149
Augustus, Emperor 70, 74
authority 17, 54, 65, 84, 86, 88, 90, 94, 104, 128

Bacall, Lauren 118
backs 46
Baker, Josephine 114
balaclavas 149
Balenciaga, Cristobal 55
Balmain, Pierre 25
Balzac, Honoré de 122, 124
Bates, John 21
bathing costumes *see* swimwear
Bathsheba 114
beading 62, 134
Beatty, Admiral 85
beauty 20, 22, 29, 75, 77, 82
Beauvoir, Simone de 101
Belville Sassoon 88
Benson, Arthur 100
Bernini, Giovanni Lorenzo 111–12
Binder, Pearl 58, 59, 109
blue jeans 25, 47–8, 52, 57, 60, 65, 125, 153, 155
body-scoring 131, 132
body-stocking 150
Boileau, Abbé 90–1
Bokassa, Emperor 86
Boleyn, Anne 82
bondage 146, 147–50
boredom 28, 148, 154
Borg, Bjorn 75–7, 78, 154
bosom *see* breasts
bottines 35
bottoms 21, 36, 39, 45–8, 62, 63, 77, 78
bows 48, 56, 66, 116, 123, 136, 137, 138–40, 154
brassière, bra 25, 103, 110, 126, 143, 154
breasts 19, 36–40, 90–1, 92, 98, 110, 118, 137
Brontë, Charlotte 110
Brooks Brothers 60
Burton, Robert 15
bustle, revival of 48
buttocks *see* bottoms
buttons 31, 92, 127, 138

Cadabra, Thea 36
Callot, Jacques 89
cami-knickers 127
Cardin, Pierre 25, 94

Carlyle, Thomas 58
Cartland, Barbara 110
Charles V, Emperor 71
Charles II, King 68, 109
Charles VIII, King 25
Charles, Prince of Wales 64, 85
Chaucer, Geoffrey 107
chests 62, 77
China 32, 34, 35, 84
Chloé 33
chopines 36
Christian Church, influence of 19, 22, 90, 91–3, 105
Cinderella 115, 116, 117
classical dress 68, 71, 72, 83, 96, 97–8
Cleopatra 49, 70, 74, 117, 150
cloche hats 16, 50
codpiece 17, 36, 83, 104, 105–6
Coignet, Sergeant 128–30
collars 55, 56, 64, 66, 95
colours 98, 133–4, 151
Connaught, Duke of 87, 100
Connaught, Duchess of 87, 100
Cooper, Lady Diana 100
corselets 55, 101
corsets 17, 32, 34, 55, 66, 99, 122, 124, 128, 131, 140, 150
Cosimo, Saint 34
Courrèges, André 139
Courtly Love 114–15
cravats 66
Creed, Charles 133
Cremers-van der Does, Eline Canter 93
Cretan priestesses 22, 32, 155
Cromwell, Oliver 109, 123
Cupid 63, 98, 106, 112

dance dress 119
Daniel 114
Darwin, Charles 18, 19
David, King 114
décolletage 52, 66, 120
de Havilland, Olivia 117
denims *see* blue jeans
Dior, Christian 17, 30, 40, 138
Disney, Walt 117
dog-collar 55
du Maurier, George 65
Duncan, Isadora 119

Edward VII, King 84
Edward VIII, King 84, 85
Elizabeth of Austria, Empress 133
Elizabeth I, Queen 38–9, 75, 83, 87
Elizabeth II, Queen 85
erogenous zones 29–57, 61, 62
espadrilles 36
Estrées, Gabrielle d' 92
Eve 18–19, 23, 91, 113, 151
executioners' dress 63, 89, 148–50

fabrics 25, 131, 133, 137
Falaise, Louise de la 88
fancy dress 100-1, 134
Fath, Jacques 53
fatness 21
feet 29, 32–6, 70, 77, 78, 98–9, 117

fertility symbols 22, 32, 43, 57, 79, 105, 151, 155
fetishism 34, 35, 63, 140, 150
fig-leaves 18, 19, 20, 23, 91
Flügel, John Carl 154, 155
Flynn, Errol 117
Fortuny y de Madrazo, Mariano 25
Freud, Sigmund 22, 38, 110, 146
frills 36, 41, 66, 103, 116
fundamentalism 17, 19, 22
fur 54, 117, 133

Gamages 104
Garbo, Greta 123-4
Gay Liberation Movement 17
George V, King 84
Gibb, Bill 125
Gibson, Charles Dana 66
girdles 136–7, 138
Givenchy, Hubert de 78, 118, 142–3, 155
gloves 26, 31, 54, 55, 94, 152
gold 86, 130
Grace of Monaco, Princess 40
Greeks 24, 51, 77, 109, 113, 154
Greenhough, Horatio 72–3
guilt 148

Hagman, Larry 81
hair 49–52; blonde 50; body 51, 63; dark 50; depilation 51–2; forearms, on 77, 80, 81; pubic 52, 104, 113
hairstyles, beehive 50; bun 51; chignon 46, 50, 51, 103; curls 18, 49; long 25, 49; punk 51, 155
hair transplants 51
hands 54
Harlow, Jean 38
Harrods 130
Hartnell, Norman 134
hats 17, 31, 80, 81, 85, 118
Hayworth, Rita 118
Henry VIII, King 82–3, 93, 117
Hepworths 58, 60
Herculaneum 24
hermaphrodites 19, 39, 40, 151
Hermes 151
heroism 68–71, 76, 80, 153
high heels 25, 36, 47, 60
Hippolyta 136
hips 57, 92
Hogarth, William 126
homosexuality 36, 103, 107
Hood, Robin 117
hoods 63, 149
hooks and eyes 143
Hope, Polly 155
hot pants 48

Indian religious art 22, 24, 34
Iphigenia 101, 106

Jaeger, Dr Gustav 66, 95, 131
James II, King 71
jeans *see* blue jeans
Jerome, Saint 91
Jesus Christ 91
jewellery 16, 41, 51, 56, 88, 114, 130
jock-straps 105

jogging shorts 48
Jung, Carl 146
Justinian, Emperor 84

Katherine of Aragon 82
Kennedy, Jaqueline 54
Kent, Duchess of 88
kilts 68, 69
kimonos 46, 113
Kissinger, Henry 86
Klein, Calvin 26
knickers 78, 122, 125, 126, 129, *see also* pants
Knox, John 107

'La Bonne' 36
lace 46, 87, 88, 100, 125, 128
lacings 56, 140, 154
Lagerfeld, Karl 33
Lawrence, D. H. 79
legs 40–3, 62, 121
lesbianism 92, 110, 150
Lespinasse, Mlle de 125, 126
lingerie 124–5, 127, 128, *see also* underwear
Logan, Andrew 151
Lolita 45, 103
Lollobrigida, Gina 40
lotus-foot shoe 34
Louis XIV, King 29, 59, 74, 90, 110
Louise of Lorraine 87
Lucie-Smith, Edward 147, 148
Lytton, Bulwer 60

McEnroe, John 75, 76
Maintenon, Madame de 29, 110
Maitland, Sir Richard 107
Marie Antoinette 101
Mark Antony 68, 70, 117
Marlborough, Duke of 68, 71–2
Marlborough, Duchess of 68, 70
Mary, Queen 55, 84
Mary, Virgin 92
Medusa 99
Midler, Bette 122, 127
military dress 74, 85, 86, 87
Ming, Sheila 21
mini-skirts 42, 43, 104, 106, 152
Missoni 25
Monroe, Marilyn 38, 47
Morris, Bernardine 26
Mother Hubbards 22, 23
Muir, Jean 138
Murillo 92

nakedness 19, 89, 91, 111, 112, 114, 121, 154
Napoleon 97, 128
naval dress 85
neck 46, 52–5, 62, 63, 66
nipples 16, 39, 56, 103
Norell, Norman 134
nudity *see* nakedness

oriental eroticism 46

padding 36, 46, 78, 79, 98, 125, 128
panti-girdles 55, 126

pants 43, 103, 129, *see also* knickers
Parat, Jean 150
Paris 24, 25, 30, 33, 40, 125, 152, 153
Parker, Dorothy 131, 134
Pearl, Una 47
peasant dress 52, 100–1, 140
pelvis 21, 35
penis 16, 34, 39, 62, 63, *see also* phallic symbolism, phallus
Perrault, Charles 115, 117
Perseus 99, 117, 145–7, 148
phallic symbolism 24, 34, 35, 57, 79, 80, 92, 106, 112, 113, 154
phallus 36, 62, 70, 105, *see also* penis
Philip II, King 98
Philip, Duke of Edinburgh 85
Pilotello line 21
Piombo, Sebastiano del 147
platform soles 36, 51, 80
Pompadour, Madame de 66, 139
power 26, 31, 59, 61, 65, 72, 73, 83, 86, 88, 94, 153, 155
press-studs 143
Pucci, Emilio 25
pudenda 39, 55–7, 106, 137
punk dress 51, 79, 141–2, 147–8
Puritan ethics 26, 39, 82, 103, 109, 111, 130, 151

Rabanne, Paco 154
Reagan, Nancy 26
Reger, Janet 123, 127
Reid and Taylor 60
Rhodes, Zandra 60, 125, 139, 151
Rooke, James 36
Rubens, Sir Peter Paul 111
Rudofsky, Bernard 45, 101
Russell, Rosalind 118

S-bend line 21, 46
Sade, Marquis de 148
sado-masochistic dress 147–50
St Laurent, Yves 40, 48, 88
Salome 114
satin 131, 134
Savile Row 58, 81, 155
scent 135
Schiaparelli, Elsa 25, 134, 140
Schulberg, Bud 35
see-through fabrics 54, 102, 103
sexual deviation 147–9
Shilling, David 17
shirts 130
shoes 17, 34, 35–6, 41, 91, 94, 105
shoulders 39, 52–3, 59, 62, 70, 77, 78, 90
silk 65, 84, 124
singlets 80
skirts 26, 41–2, 48, 68, 93, 105, 120
slashed dress 62, 141–2
Sleeping Beauty 115, 116, 117
sleeves 17, 80, 81
slimness 62, 66–7
Smith, Adam 87
Snow White 17, 115, 116, 117, 118
Spencer, Lady Diana *see* Wales, Princess of

spine 46
sporran 106
Staël, Madame de 110
stockings 43, 104, 122, 127, 129, 142, 149
stocking tops 41, 42, 129
stomach 32, 55–7, 62
style 45, 75
Suckling, Sir John 35
suits, three-piece 17, 58–60, 64, 81, 90, 119, 149, 152
suspenders 17
sweater dress 47
swimwear 21, 103, 104

T-shirts 25, 57, 93, 152
tattooes 56, 80, 131, 132
tennis dress 75–8, 104
Teresa, Saint 111–12
testicles 19, 62
Thatcher, Margaret 122–3
thighs 41, 42, 55–7, 103, 106, 120
Thomas, Earl of Lancaster 151
tights 43, 106, 122, 152
Tinling, Teddy 78, 130
Titian 71
topless dress 39, 105, 110
Topolski, Felix 86
transvestitism 66, 101–2, 123, 150–1
Travolta, John 57
Treu, Martin 149
Trevelyan, George Macaulay 60
trousers 17, 57, 68
trouser-suits 57
Turnbull and Asser 130

underwear 68, 69, 91, 95, 122–30, *see also* lingerie
uniforms 65–6, 74–5, 79, 85, 86

vagina 34, 39, 117, 147
Valentino 25, 140
vanity 67
Velcro 143–4
Venus 136–7, *see also* Aphrodite
Victoria, Queen 89
Villars, Duchesse de 92
virginity 31, 39, 103, 133, 136–7, 138
virility 17, 49, 59, 67, 71, 72, 106, 119, 135, 138
Vulcan 136–7

Wade, Virginia 103
waists 22, 29, 31–2, 71, 77, 78, 91, 92
Wales, Princess of 53, 55, 110
Walpole, Horace 101
Ward, Rowland 100
Washington, George 72–3
West, Mae 38, 45
Westwood, Vivienne 151
wigs 49, 71, 73, 152
wrists 54–5

Yeats, W. B. 134
Yuki 123, 155

zips 140–3

157